THE SERGER'S
TECHNIQUE BIBLE

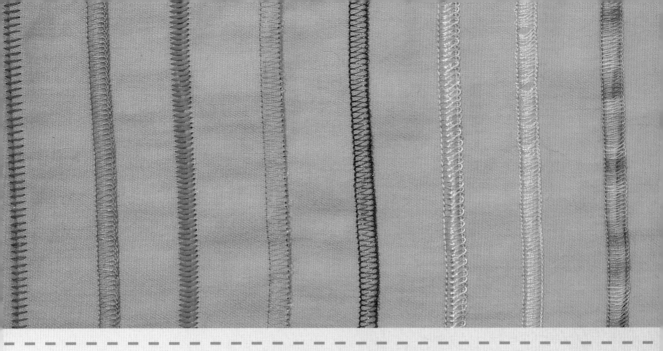

THE SERGER'S
TECHNIQUE BIBLE

From hemming and seaming to decorative stitching,
get the best from your machine

Julia Hincks

St. Martin's Griffin
New York

THE SERGER'S TECHNIQUE BIBLE

A Quarto Book
Copyright © 2014 Quarto Inc.
All rights reserved.

Printed in China. For information, address
St. Martin's Press, 175 Fifth Avenue,
New York, N.Y. 10010.

www.stmartins.com

Library of Congress Cataloging-in-Publication
Data Available Upon Request

ISBN: 978-1-250-04272-9

St. Martin's Griffin books may be purchased for
educational, business, or promotional use. For
information on bulk purchases, please contact
Macmillan Corporate and Premium Sales
Department at 1-800-221-7945, extension 5442,
or write specialmarkets@macmillan.com.

First Edition: April 2014

10 9 8 7 6 5 4 3 2 1

Conceived, designed, and produced by
Quarto Publishing plc
The Old Brewery
6 Blundell Street
London N7 9BH

QUAR.SSMB

Project Editor: Lily de Gatacre
Art Editor and Designer: Julie Francis
Photographer: Simon Pask
Copyeditor: Sally MacEachern
Proofreader: Sarah Hoggett
Illustrator: Kuo Kang Chen
Indexer: Ann Barrett
Art Director: Caroline Guest

Creative Director: Moira Clinch
Publisher: Paul Carslake

Color separation in Hong Kong by Cypress
Colors (HK) Ltd.
Printed in China by 1010 Printing Limited

Contents

About this book

A serger can seem a little daunting at first but once you've used one and got to grips with it, you will never look back. No more conventional zigzag to edge your seam allowances—these machines will give your home-sewing projects a more professional finish. In this book you will see just how easy your machine can be to thread up and sew, edging your fabrics quickly and creating a perfect finish to any project. Step-by-step instructions ensure that you set your tensions and differential feed dials correctly to get the best results with any fabric.

TYPES OF MACHINE
This book is appropriate for most makes and types of serger, from two-thread through to five-thread machines.

CHAPTER 1
SERGING BASICS PAGES 10–43

This part looks under the serger's hood and shows you how to set up your machine, get the tension just right, and get off to a flying start by choosing the right tools, threads, and textiles.

MEASUREMENTS
Measurements are given in both imperial and metric. All conversions are approximate, so follow either imperial or metric.

Tips and troubleshooting panels provide shortcuts for the best method to adopt and suggest ways to fix errors.

Large-format step-by-steps are easy to follow.

Enlargements go in tight on finished seams and edges to show the stitch in more detail.

CHAPTER 2
TECHNIQUES PAGES 44–95

This section explains all of the core techniques you need for professional serging results, illustrated with clear step-by-step photography for ease of use and clarity.

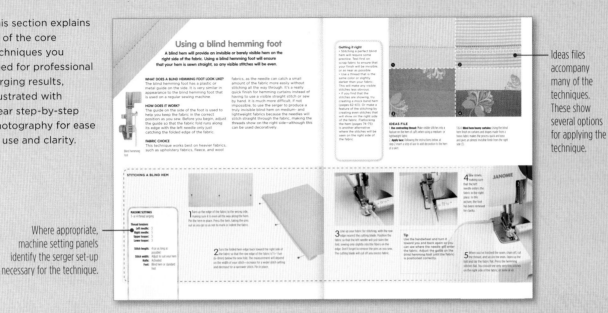

Ideas files accompany many of the techniques. These show several options for applying the technique.

Where appropriate, machine setting panels identify the serger set-up necessary for the technique.

CHAPTER 3
QUICK CONSTRUCTIONS PAGES 96–119

Practical serger uses to speed up your dressmaking and project construction time; this part has a good range of projects to put your new-found skills into practice.

GUIDE TO FABRICS
For a guide to machine settings depending on the fabrics you are using, turn to page 120.

Step-by-steps walk you through the process.

You Will Need panel lists all the tools and equipment necessary to create each project.

Why I love my serger

I have to admit I was a bit scared when I first got a serger—so many threads, so many dials…where do I start? Thankfully it wasn't as hard as I thought— I just needed to have a go.

Before I owned a serger, I had spent years trying to perfect my finishing techniques— edge finishing my seams with zigzag, or using pinking shears. I was never happy with the results; although pinking shears made the fabric edge look pretty, eventually fraying would appear and spoil the insides of my garments. Projects finished with zigzag had similar problems and looked scrappy. I always felt that my creations looked obviously hand made and unprofessional.

PERFECT SEAMS
I couldn't believe the difference when I started using my serger. No more fraying on seam allowances! I could even finish hems with the serger, which is brilliant for fabrics that are difficult to work with, such as silks and sheer fabrics. I'd almost given up trying to work with jerseys and knitted fabrics, as my seams ended up puckered or fraught with missed stitches, but the serger sewed these perfectly. The serger really has changed my life—well, at least the way I sew!

SHARING MY LOVE OF SERGERS
I knew my students would love the finish, too: they were often unhappy about edge finishing their seam allowances and the results they ended up with. So I introduced my students to the serger. I demonstrated how to make a simple seam on the sewing machine and then finished the seam allowance with the serger. They watched as I fed the fabric under the foot, let the blade cut off the fraying edge, and allowed the machine to edge finish the fabric with stitches. I passed the finished seam around the class to the sounds of "ooh," "wow," "that's so easy,"…"can I have a go?"…"what's that machine called again?"…"I want one!" After that, they all wanted to use the serger to finish their projects.

So now, throughout the pages of this book, I hope I can take you on that same exciting journey that I took my students, and show you how the serger can open up a whole new world of sewing and finishing. From learning simple techniques to decorative edgings and quick constructions, I hope you'll find something to turn your serger into your new best friend.

Serged seams, facing, and hem on this skirt give a professional, finished look.

Use contrasting colors for the edge finishing on the inside of a denim skirt.

Classic stitched hems work well on heavy fabrics.

Rolled hems make nice clean edges.

Makes a nice decorative finish for frilly edges.

Serged seams prevent fraying fabrics.

Great for lettuce-effect edging for tops and dresses.

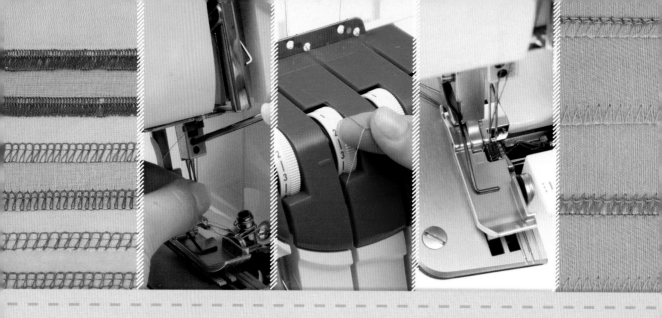

CHAPTER 1
Serging Basics

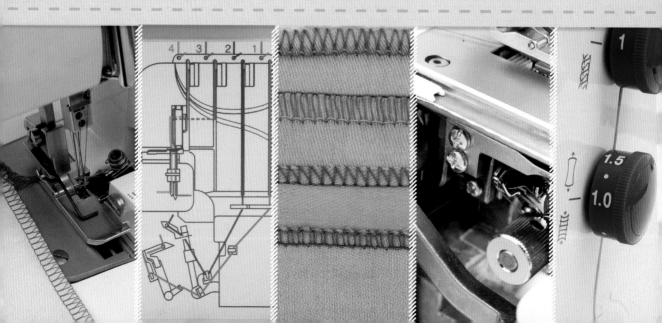

So you've got a serger—what now? This chapter will guide you through all the basics, so by the end of it you'll be set up and ready to serge with confidence. We kick off by examining all the components that you can expect to find on your machine, as well as taking a look at some invaluable tools. You'll find detailed information about how to set up your machine and serge those first stitches, how to fix mistakes, and how to finish. Finally, there's a section that will introduce you to all the adjustable settings on your serger, and teach you when and how to adjust them, in order to perfect your stitches and get the best out of your serger.

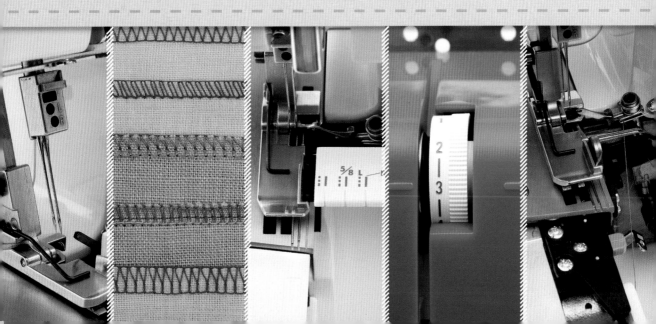

Anatomy of a serger

All serger machines have the same basic features and can be set up and used in the same or a very similar way. Even if you don't have the model shown here, your machine will most likely have the same parts in the same place that will do the same thing.

Differences between models

In terms of appearance, the main difference between models is the position of the thread tension dials. In some models they are integrated into the top of the front of the machine, whereas in other models they are knobs on the front of the machine. Don't worry—they all do the same thing!

Other differences in the features of the most basic or introductory-level machines are the number of threads the machine can hold at one time—for example, 2-, 3-, 4-, or 5-thread serging—and the range of differential feed, stitch width, and cutting width settings.

❶ Needles

This serger has two needles, but can be used with just one for a narrower stitch length and finer serging. The needles used are HA-1 SP no. 11 and 14. Each machine will recommend a type of needle to use for the best results. The needle has a flat part and a curved part at the top. The flat part will be positioned to the back of the needle holder.

❷ Needle clamp screws

Secure needles in place by tightening the needle clamp screws with a screwdriver. This ensures that the needle does not work its way loose, causing it to break or to damage the machine.

❸ Needle plate

The needle plate provides a smooth surface to pass the fabric under the foot of the machine. There is a hole in it for the needle and the feed dog teeth. Ensure that the plate is kept clean and free of oil or dirt. Unlike the sewing machine, there are usually no stitching guidelines on the needle plate of a serger.

❹ Presser foot

A basic serger foot is provided with the machine—most types of serging can be done with this foot. Additional feet for specialist techniques can be purchased as accessories (see pages 79–95).

❺ Presser foot lever

This allows the presser foot to be lifted up and down. Access it with the left hand, reaching around the outside and to the back of the presser foot. For most basic serging, the presser foot can remain in the lowered position.

❻ Stitching guidelines

To the right of the needle plate, on top of the looper cover, you may find stitching guidelines. They help to keep your stitching straight when you sew. Here they are marked with "L" and "R" to show the distance from the left- and right-hand needles.

❼ Feed dogs

These are found below the presser foot. On a serger there are two sets of teeth, which work with the differential feed. The teeth work independently of each other, one at the front guiding the fabric under the foot toward the needle and one at the rear of the machine taking the fabric from behind the needle.

❽ Knife

This trims the edge of the fabric, creating a neat, clean edge free of fraying threads. There are usually separate upper and lower knife blades. On this model, the upper knife can be kept in position or lowered out of the way when it is not required. To lower the knife, open the side and looper covers and push in the upper knife adjusting knob (usually found to the left of the needle plate). This will push the knife out to the right and away from the needle plate. Carefully turn the knob toward you, bringing the knife down. Release the knob. The lower knife has a fixed position, but only cuts when used in conjunction with the upper knife. They can both be replaced when blunt.

❾ Differential feed

Not all machines have this feature, but it is present on the majority of introductory-level machines. It may be a dial or a lever. The differential feed works in conjunction with the feed dog teeth and can be used to eliminate unwanted gathering, stretching, or puckering on seams and hems. It can also be used to create gathers and stretch where required. Here, the numbers on the differential feed show the ratio of speeds between front and back teeth. All machines have a neutral position where the speed of front and back feed dog teeth is equal—in this case, 1.0. A higher number would indicate the front teeth moving more quickly than the back teeth, which would create a gathered effect on the fabric. Conversely, a lower number on the differential feed dial would indicate the front teeth moving more slowly than the back, creating stretching at the edge of the fabric.

❿ Spool pins

This machine has four spool pins situated at the back of the machine on the spool stand. Other machines may only have two or three, while some models have up to 10! The spools can sit directly on the pins or they can be used with spool holders, which allow larger spools to sit more comfortably, without falling off the back of the spool stand or rattling around as the machine is used.

⓫ Tension dials

When you are threading up the machine, each thread will have its own tension dial. This controls how tightly or loosely the thread is held and pulled through the machine. The dials may be built-in on the top front of the machine or knobs on the front of the machine. This model has the built-in dials. Generally, for basic serging, the threads will all be set to the neutral position. On this model the neutral position is to have all thread dials at 3. They can then be tightened (higher number) or loosened (lower number) according to the threads and fabrics being used, or to enable a desired technique or stitch finish.

⓬ Thread guides

These hold the thread in place as it goes from the spool to a needle or to a looper. As the machine is threaded, each thread will have a set path to ensure the correct use of the machine; if a thread is out of its guide, you may have problems with irregular stitching or snapping. Take most care on the lower looper, as often thread guides here are missed, which results in frustration when the stitches aren't formed correctly or the threads break.

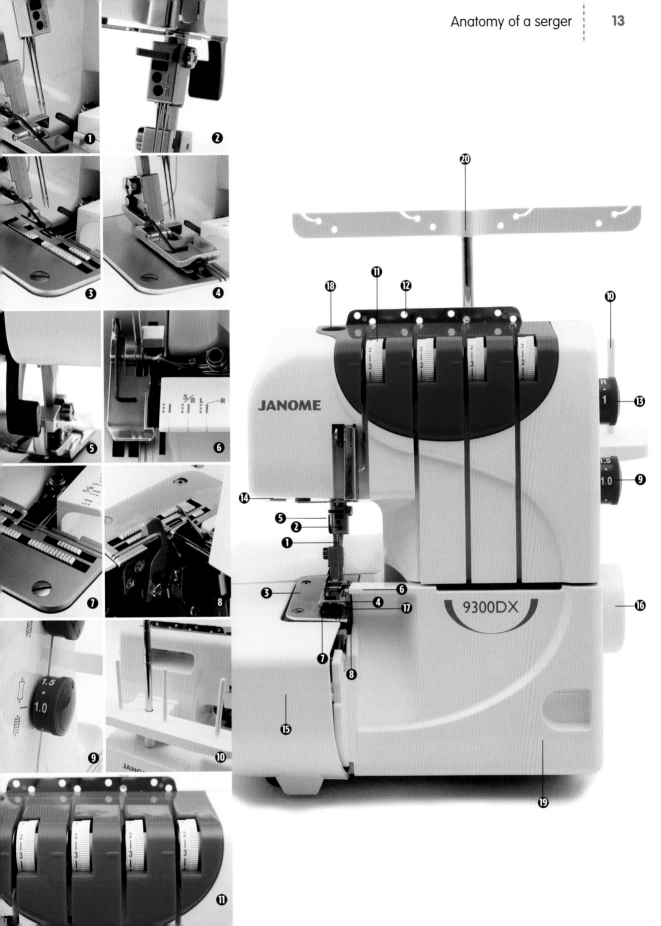

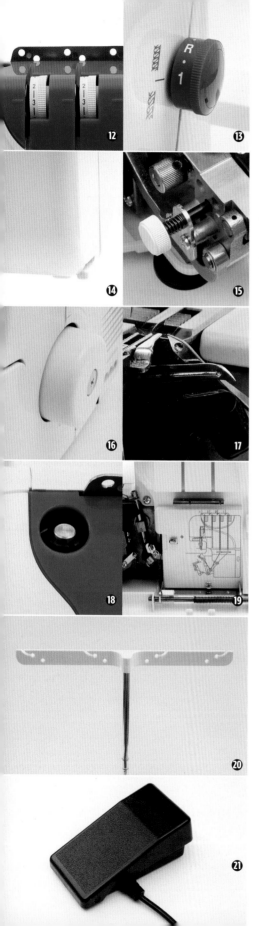

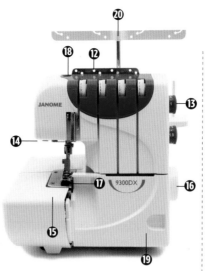

On most models, the thread guides are color coded so you can see a clear pathway for the thread. The machine may need to be threaded in a given order to ensure that it runs smoothly.

⑬ Stitch length
This can be adjusted with a dial or a lever. On this model, the dial is on the right-hand side. For most mediumweight fabrics, the stitch length should be set to 2.5. For heavier fabrics this can be made longer by changing the dial to a higher number, whereas for finer fabrics the stitch can be made shorter by setting to a lower number.

⑭ Thread cutter
On the left-hand side of the machine will be a thread cutter. It allows quick and easy cutting of the threads without having to reach for the scissors. If the cutter is not on the left of the machine, look behind the needle or on the presser foot lever. Leave a long enough tail before cutting the threads or you may find that you need to rethread your machine. Keep the thread cutter free from loose threads, as it may become blunt.

⑮ Adjustable cutting width
Adjust the cutting width on your machine by moving the upper knife blade away from or toward the needle plate. This can help overcome stitching problems where loops form on the edge of the fabric. On this model, you turn a white dial inside the left side cover to change the cutting width. Other models may have the dial on the outside of the machine.

⑯ Handwheel
On the right of the machine is the handwheel. It can be turned to move the position of the needles and loopers when changing the needle or threading the machine. As a general rule, always turn the handwheel toward you.

⑰ Stitch finger
This can be found on the needle plate. The serging stitch forms around the stitch finger and the formed stitch feeds off the end of the finger. This is clearer to see when serging without fabrics. To enable narrower stitching or rolled hemming, the stitch finger can usually be disengaged and move.

⑱ Foot pressure adjuster
On some machine models, you have the option of adjusting the pressure the foot has on the fabrics. For most fabrics, this adjustment is not necessary. For heavier fabrics, less pressure may be needed and so the pressure can be adjusted accordingly. For lighter fabrics, more pressure may be needed and so the pressure is adjusted to suit.

⑲ Looper cover
To thread the machine, you will need to open the looper cover. On many models there is a color-coded threading guide inside. If you refer to this as you thread, you won't have to reach for your machine manual or seek additional help. Ensure that the inside of the looper cover is kept clean and free of lint, as this can affect the tension on the looper threads. Some machines have a safety feature that stops the machine from working if the looper cover is open.

⑳ Thread guide bar
This keeps the threads untangled as they travel from the spool to the needles or loopers. This bar can be extended and should be raised up to its highest position to allow the threads to travel smoothly.

㉑ Foot pedal
All machines will come with a foot pedal. The harder you press, the faster the machine goes. On some foot pedals you can change the speed setting to high or low, allowing you to work more slowly or more quickly, depending on your preference.

ADDITIONAL FEATURES OF MID- TO HIGH-RANGE MACHINES

Mid- to high-range sergers often have several additional features to those listed on the previous pages. Not every machine will include all of the features listed.

❶ Automatic tension settings

On machines that offer a range of different stitches some models have automatic tension setting so that, no matter which stitch program you choose, the machine will automatically choose the tension for the best results. No need for tinkering with the tension dials to get the stitch to look the way you want it.

❷ Cover stitch and chain stitch settings

On basic machines these aren't usually an option, but for more expensive machines you can change the stitch settings to create a chain stitch or cover stitch. This usually involves changing the settings on the machine, as well as moving the needles and sometimes changing the needle plate or looper cover. If you use these stitches frequently, you may wish to invest in a separate machine that only does chain or cover stitches.

❸ Tension release device

This is more common on machines offering chain stitch or cover stitch settings. When you have finished stitching the fabric, it is not advisable to continue sewing chain or cover stitch without any fabric under the foot. Instead, stop sewing and hold the tension release button. The fabric can then be pulled clear of the machine and the threads cut.

❹ Additional spool pins

Basic sergers will work for two, three, or four spools. More advanced machines can cater for a wider range of stitch lengths, widths, and types, and work with up to ten spools.

Waste tray

This useful tray may come with your serger. It will catch all the bits of thread and fabrics that the knife cuts off, saving you clearing-up time after your sewing sessions. Some brands sell separate waste trays that can be fitted under the front legs of the machine, but a plastic bag will do the job just as well.

Free arm

Sometimes the sewing space is a little tight on machines when you are trying to serge hems on sleeves, especially when making clothing for children. Some models offer a free arm, like that on a regular sewing machine, where a part of the front of the machine can be removed to allow you to stitch small tubular items.

Extra height on the presser foot

When sewing through thicker fabrics, it is often desirable to raise the foot higher than it may sometimes wish to go. More advanced machines offer this extra height, enabling you to get more layers of fabric under the foot, or indeed to sew through heavier fabrics such as denims and tweeds.

Safety no-sew system

On some advanced machines, the power locks out when the presser foot is lifted or the cover is open. This means that the machine won't stitch until the cover is closed and the presser foot is lowered.

Easy thread system

More expensive models may offer self-threading or an airflow threading system. While these sound like fantastic alternatives to becoming frustrated with threading your machine, they do come at a price. So it might be worth working out how to thread your basic machine to avoid blowing your budget.

Built-in storage

Some standard sergers enable you to store useful tools and accessories in a storage compartment within the machine. Other models come with an accessory box for you to keep tools in, or are sold with additional accessories in a storage bag.

Tilting needle clamp

Needles on a serger can be more difficult to replace than on a standard machine, since they are so close together and in a tight space. Certain serger models have introduced a tilting needle clamp, which allows you to tilt the needles toward you, making it easier to change needles or move the needle position.

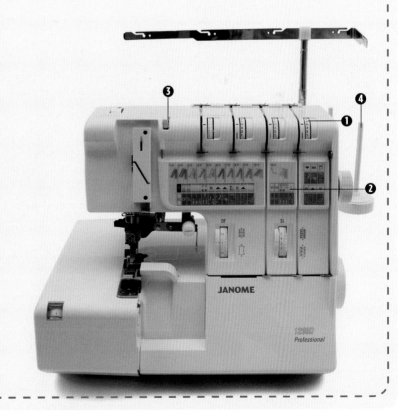

JANOME

Must-have tools

Most sewers will have a range of general sewing items, which you will need to have close at hand for any sewing task. This list covers the main items you will need for any sewing project.

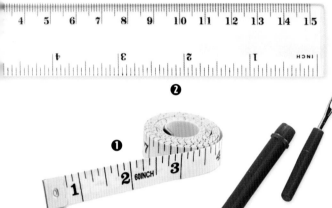

Essential beginner's kit
The range of tools on the market can be intimidating and there's no need to buy everything at once. Start with this suggested beginner's kit.

- Thread snips or small scissors
- Tape measure
- Fabric scissors
- Quick unpick tool
- Tailor's chalk
- Tweezers
- Screwdriver
- Lint brush

MEASURING TOOLS
❶ Tape measure It's best to have one that has both inches and centimeters, as some patterns and project instructions will use one or the other. They are generally 60in (150cm) in length. Tape measures can stretch over time, so be sure to replace old ones to keep measurements accurate.

❷ Rules A sturdy metal or plastic rule with inches and centimeters is invaluable when drawing patterns or marking fabric. Pattern cutting or patchwork rulers are excellent for sewing projects, as they are usually longer and wider and can act as a weight to keep the fabric flat and also to stop it from slipping while marking out.

SCISSORS AND CUTTING TOOLS
❸ Fabric scissors These come in a range of weights and sizes and are priced for every budget, from heavy tailoring shears at the top end to more reasonably priced lightweight dressmaking scissors. Scissors with cushioned holes allow for more comfortable cutting. Label them "fabric only," as they will blunt very quickly if used as general-purpose

household scissors. You should have a separate pair of scissors for cutting paper and anything that isn't fabric.

❹ Thread snips or small scissors A smaller pair of scissors is handy for trimming threads once you have finished at the sewing machine or serger. When threading or rethreading your machine, they also come in useful for cutting fraying thread ends so that you have a clean, sharp end to get through the needles or loopers.

❺ Pinking shears These scissors with zigzag edges are great for cutting out pieces of fabric that you don't want to fray. They are also ideal for finishing seam allowances, especially on short seams or areas where it is hard to serge. Pinking shears don't stop all fabrics from fraying, however, and work best on cottons or cotton blends.

❻ Quick unpick tool The most frequently used tool in the sewing box for any beginner. It resembles a two-prong fork with a curved blade between the prongs for cutting. Unpickers generally come in two sizes—the smaller

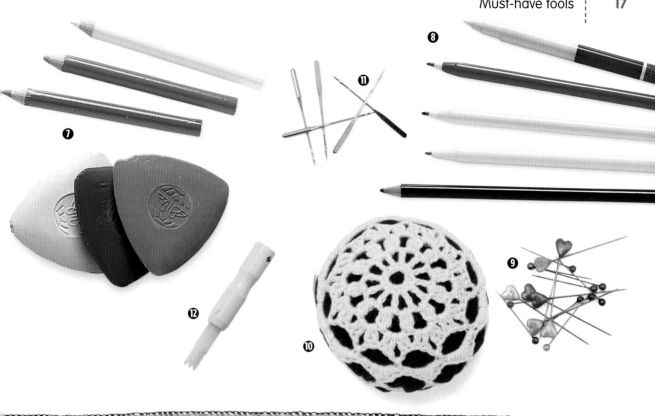

one is better for more precision in cutting stitches instead of making unwanted holes in fabrics.

MARKING TOOLS

7 Tailor's chalk This comes as handy sharpenable pencils or as blocks of chalk in a variety of colors, so you can usually find one that will show up on your chosen fabric. It is great for marking fabrics, and can be brushed away or washed off. It can be hard to mark certain fabrics or places precisely, especially when working with jersey fabrics. Don't iron the chalk markings—this will set the chalk into the fabric and it may never come off!

8 Vanishing marker pens Mark onto your fabrics with pen—don't worry, it will wash out or fade over time. These pens allow greater marking precision than chalks, but some fade almost immediately, so only use this type of marker if you intend to make use of those marks straightaway.

9 Pins Use pins for marking sections of fabric, as well as for keeping fabrics together. Pins come in different thicknesses, lengths, and styles, so choose the right ones for your fabric and needs. Longer pins with glass or plastic heads are great for pinning out patterns onto fabrics, and dropped pins can be spotted easily. Some fabrics can be damaged by thicker pins, so try to keep the pins within the seam allowance at the edge of pattern pieces—5/8in (1.5cm)—so that any damage will not be seen on a finished garment. Keep pins away from the serger blades as, unlike with sewing machines, serging over pins will blunt the blade.

10 Pincushion Keep your pins stored safely in a pincushion. Magnetic pin trays are also available and are great for collecting discarded pins from the floor.

NEEDLES AND NEEDLE THREADER

11 Serger needles Serger needles are specially designed to work on a range of fabrics, including jerseys and knits, and will eliminate skipped stitches as you sew. Using general-purpose sewing machine needles may work on some models, but each machine will recommend a type of needle to use. If you misplace your manual, then look at the needles currently in the machine and use these. Using the wrong needle can cause a series of problems—from uneven or skipped stitches to damage to the loopers. Needles should be changed regularly—not just once they break. Needles will become blunt after time and will wear out more when sewing certain fabrics, especially synthetic fibers such as polyester, metallic fabrics, and fur fabrics.

12 Needle threader A useful little tool for when you have trouble threading needles, either on the machine or when hand sewing. The most common design is a small tinned plate with a triangle of metal wire attached. Push the metal loop through the eye of the needle from back to front, if using the serger, then insert thread though the metal loop and pull this back through the needle. Other types of needle threaders are available and may come with your machine. These can be inserted from front to back through the machine needle.

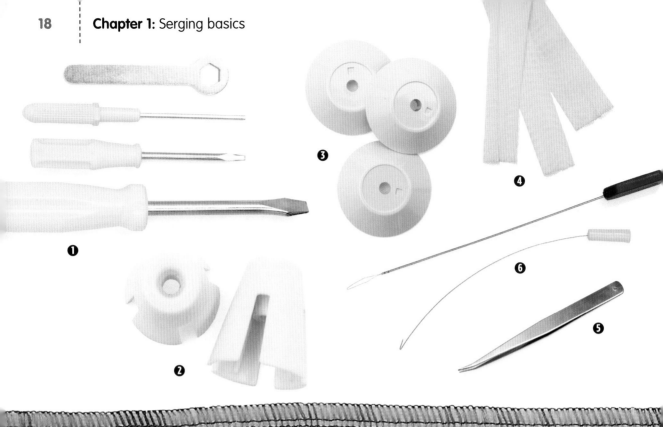

SERGING TOOLS

❶ Screwdrivers Your serger should come with a screwdriver set. You may not need it straight away, but keep it safe for future use. These tools will prove essential for loosening and tightening the needle clamp screws when replacing the needles. Some machines come with a specific spanner or Allen key style tool. Sometimes screws may work themselves loose with the vibrations of the machine. Always check that the stoppers underneath the machine are tightened up and the screws on the needle plate are secure.

❷ Spool holder or adapter These are great for stabilizing larger thread cones and stopping them from rattling around. If you find they're not working for you and the rattling of spools continues, try putting the spool holders onto the spool pins upside down. These holders can be removed when using smaller spools of thread.

❸ Spool cap Use one of these to stop smaller spools of thread from moving around too much. They also allow the thread to ravel smoothly. Most spool caps are wider than the spool itself and so are great for parallel-wound spools that have nicks in the top. These nicks, usually used for securing thread when the spool is not in use, can cause the thread to get caught when serging and then snap.

❹ Spool nets A great accessory for decorative threads such as silks. Place the net over the spool to stop unnecessary unwinding or tangling of the thread. If the net is longer than the spool, fold the net down so that threads don't catch on the ends of the net. These nets can also be used when the thread is not in use for tangle-free storage.

❺ Tweezers A must-have for threading lower loopers and hard-to-reach thread guides. Most sergers will come with a pair of tweezers—keep them safe and on hand when using your serger.

❻ Looper threader This can look similar to a needle threader and is a tool with a small metal looper hook at one end. Use it in the same way as the needle threader by inserting the metal loop from back to front through the looper, passing the thread through the metal loop, and then pulling it through the looper. This tool is ideal when threading woolly nylon or thicker threads through the upper and lower loopers. Make your own looper threader using a length of brightly colored thread. Fold the thread in half and twist these ends together. Push these ends through the looper, leaving the loop of thread hanging out. Insert your serging thread through your brightly colored thread loop and pull on the twisted ends, bringing the serging thread through the looper.

❼ Bodkin A bodkin is a needle with a large eye. They are sometimes sold as hand embroidery needles for children and may be plastic or metal with a blunt tip. Bodkins are great for finishing off the ends of serging. Pass serged thread ends through the eye of the bodkin and then push the tip of the bodkin through a short section of stitching on the fabric. Pull through and cut off any threads that are not now encased in the serged fabric.

❽ Loop turner Used in the same way as the bodkin for finishing ends of serging, this tool is usually used for turning through stitching and seams to the right side when creating rouleau loops or skinny straps for clothing, bags, or other household items.

Seam and thread sealants (not shown) A wide variety of thread and seam sealants are available and all are great at stopping seams from fraying or serger chains from raveling. Use them sparingly

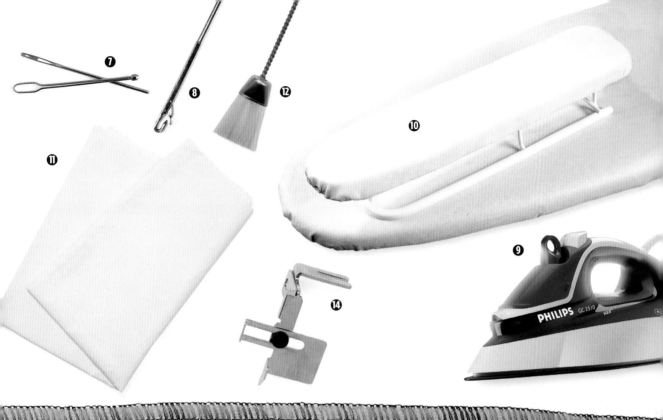

and always test a section first. Sometimes they can leave a hard lump, which may not be desired on some projects.

PRESSING EQUIPMENT

9 Iron and ironing board A good steam iron is essential for pressing seams on garments and other items as they are constructed. You must press as you go. Pressing seams will help them to sit flat before they are stitched across again and will also embed stitches into fabrics so that the stitching lies flatter. Take care with heat settings and test first. Keep your iron and ironing board clean and free from burnt-on stains. Using an additional fabric cover over your ironing board cover can keep it cleaner for longer.

10 Sleeve board This is perfect for pressing seams of sleeves and pant legs, or just for small pieces of ironing when you don't want to get out your larger ironing board.

11 Pressing cloth A good item to have on hand when ironing—ideal for delicate fabrics and decorative threads. A damp pressing cloth is also great for applying certain types of interfacing.

CLEANING TOOLS

12 Lint brush This often comes as an additional accessory when purchasing a serger. It is important to keep your serger free from lint, dust, and fluff build-up when sewing, as this can clog the machine and cause problems with stitching. If your machine doesn't come with a lint brush, a household paintbrush will do the job. And if you use one with a larger head, it can remove the dust more quickly.

13 Compressed air Perfect for getting dust out of hard-to-reach places. Once most of the dust, lint, and cut fabric have been removed with a brush, use a can of compressed air to clean away any other areas you can't reach.

ADDITIONAL EXTRAS

Bob 'n' serge (not shown) If you are short on threads in matching colors, wind threads onto sewing-machine bobbins. Some bobbins will fit on the spool pins of the serger, but others are too narrow and won't fit. This handy device will fit onto a spool pin and can hold up to six bobbins.

Sidewinder (not shown) Use this device to wind threads onto bobbins without having to get out your sewing machine.

Super trim catcher (not shown) Excellent if your serger didn't come with a waste tray. This will fit most machines, hooking under the front legs of the machine.

Portable thread stand (not shown) Some larger spools may not fit on the serger without interfering with the cone next to them. Use a portable thread stand for these spools to ensure that the thread is fed evenly and untangles through the machine. This is also a great accessory if you want to use your large cone threads on a sewing machine.

14 Cloth guide An additional accessory to attach to your serger, this will help you keep your seams straight while sewing.

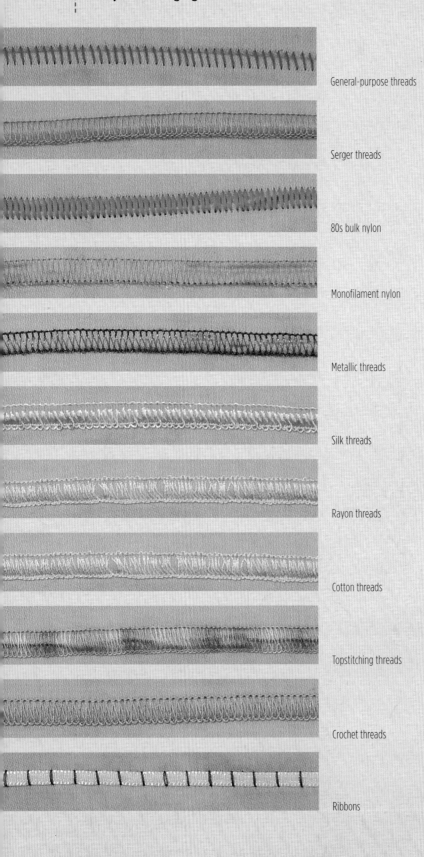

General-purpose threads

Serger threads

80s bulk nylon

Monofilament nylon

Metallic threads

Silk threads

Rayon threads

Cotton threads

Topstitching threads

Crochet threads

Ribbons

Threads

A serger will use much more thread than a regular sewing machine, especially on the loopers. You may be tempted to purchase the cheapest threads, but this may result in them snapping or in excessive lint in your machine. Here is a guide to the many different threads available for use with your serger.

General-purpose threads
These threads are ideal for both the sewing machine and the serger and can be purchased in a range of sizes and colors. They are often sold cheaply in the supermarket, but you do get what you pay for. Threads may be 100 percent polyester, polyester covered with cotton, or 100 percent cotton. This thread will suit any purpose or sewing project, as it is strong and durable.

Serger threads
These are slightly finer than general-purpose threads and are available cross-wound on cones in a range of colors. Using finer threads will reduce the bulkiness of seams. Serger threads are designed to be smoother than general-purpose threads and are more suitable for fast movement through thread guides.

80s bulk nylon
Also commonly known as woolly nylon, this thread is soft, but strong and durable. It will give excellent coverage over the edge of fabric or seams and allow some stretch, too. This thread can be used in both the needle and looper, but due to its fluffy nature it can cause problems with regular feeding through thread guides and needles. For ease of use, thread it only through the loopers. It is excellent for use on stretch fabrics, including lingerie and swimwear. It can also be used as a decorative thread finish for ruffles or other projects. Take care when ironing this thread; it will melt if the iron is too hot!

Silk threads
This luxurious thread will add shine and shimmer to projects. It is an expensive product, so use only on the loopers or as needle thread to make the silk go further. Some polyester or rayon threads can be used as an alternative to silk, as they can have a similar appearance. Due to its slipperiness, silk thread is best used with a spool net.

Rayon threads
Also known as viscose rayon or art silk, this thread has a lovely sheen and works well as a decorative thread. When used in the needles it may have a tendency to break, as it is not as strong as other threads. Thicker threads are best used in the loopers only.

Cotton threads
Heavier cotton threads can have a silklike luster, but are less expensive than silk. They can provide detail in stitching when used in the needle or loopers.

Topstitching threads
Sometimes known as buttonhole twist, this is usually a polyester thread that is thicker and stronger than general-purpose sewing thread. It has a high luster and works well for decorative use.

Crochet threads
Usually a mercerized cotton or pearl cotton, this thread is much thicker than your usual sewing thread and is available in many colors. As it is so thick it is not suitable for the needles, but can be used in the upper looper of the serger to create a braidlike decorative edge. Other yarns can also be used in the upper looper so long as they will feed evenly and are not too thick, lumpy, or fluffy.

Ribbons
Only the finest or most pliable ribbons can be used—and only in the upper looper, as the thread guides won't allow such a wide material through them. Like crochet thread, skinny ribbons can create a braidlike edge finish on seams or fabric edges. Thicker ribbons can be used to embellish flatlocking by threading through the stitching.

Woolly polyester
Useful for a range of projects to give good coverage on fabric and seam edges, woolly polyester threads are less frizzy than woolly nylon and are easier to thread. Polyester can also endure more heat and won't discolor or become brittle over time.

Monofilament nylon
A transparent, almost invisible thread, it can be used to color match any project. It comes in smoke or natural colors and can be purchased in different weights, from very fine up to a fishing-wire thickness. The finest thread has more use for a range of projects. As with woolly nylon thread take care when ironing, as it will melt. Nylon also has a tendency to yellow or become brittle over time. Substitute polyester for this fiber and you won't have these problems.

Monofilament polyester
A transparent, almost invisible thread that, unlike nylon, will withstand heat and not discolor or become brittle with time. It comes in smoke or natural colors and can be used to color match any project. This thread is soft and pliable and will lie flat once sewn.

Metallic threads
Excellent for decorative uses, these threads come in a range of thicknesses. They can be thicker than general-purpose threads and so you may have trouble getting them through the eye of the serger needles and then having a continuous flow of thread through the needle. Use this thread in the needles if it will fit, or only on the loopers, to add some sparkle and embellishment to your seams and edge finishing.

Tips
• You don't need to buy three or four cones of every color; you can make use of the threads you already have. Wind thread onto sewing-machine bobbins and use these. The handy bob 'n' serge gadget will work well if your bobbins won't fit onto the spool pins.
• Since the loopers will use more thread, alternate the use of threads for loopers and needles to make sure that the looper threads don't run out completely.
• Use heavy threads in the upper looper only.
• Inspect your thread before you buy it. Quality thread is formed of a continuous twisted fiber. If your thread looks fuzzy, with short strands sticking out, it is most likely a poor-quality thread made up of short fibers. This won't be as strong and will break frequently.

Selecting a spool
Cross-wound spools are more serger friendly, as they are designed to be unwound from the top. Parallel-wound spools are made so that the thread winds from the side—this isn't a problem, since most sergers will come with spool caps that can be fitted to allow parallel-wound spools to unwind evenly from the top.

Setting up the machine

It's time to dust off the box and get out your serger. It's not as hard as you may think to get started. If you have been worrying about how to thread the needles and loopers, chances are that once you look in the box you'll find that your serger is pre-threaded. These pages will give you guidance on threading up a three- or four-thread basic machine, but you may need to refer to your manual for model specifics, as not all machines are the same.

GETTING STARTED

The first step is to clear a space on your table and ensure that the platform is flat and won't become damaged. For more delicate surfaces, place a towel or heavy piece of fabric under your machine to absorb the vibrations or to avoid scratching or indenting the surface below. Connect the machine to the power supply and place the foot pedal on the floor. It is best to thread the machine while it is switched off—just in case your foot ends up on the foot pedal and you accidentally begin to sew! However, it is usually much easier to see the eyes of the needles with the machine light on, so if you do decide to turn the machine on, be careful! You may need to attach the thread guide bar to the back of the machine if it is not already attached. Pull up the bar so it is in its highest position. Some thread guide bars have stoppers or a system to lock the bar into position.

Choose your threads and place these on the spool pins. For parallel-wound thread, use spool caps to ensure even unwinding and avoid catching the thread on the nicks or slits in the top of the spool. Use the spool holders to stop larger cones from rattling around. If your machine is color coded, you may find it easier to use threads in the same color, as this will help you to see where to pass each thread. It may also help if you encounter problems with stitching. Turn the tension dials to the neutral position or middle tension setting—for this machine, it is set to 3. This may be highlighted in a different color on the dial or the numbers circled.

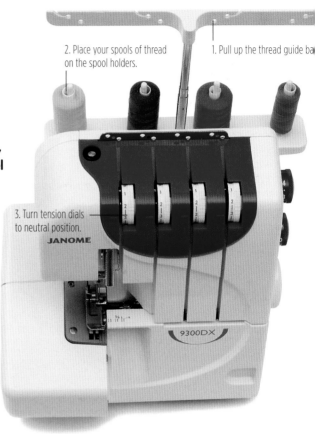

2. Place your spools of thread on the spool holders.

1. Pull up the thread guide bar

3. Turn tension dials to neutral position.

JANOME

9300DX

THREADING THE UPPER LOOPER

Follow the color coding or symbols to thread up your machine. Start with the upper looper, following the method described here.

1 Wind the handwheel so that the upper looper is almost in its highest position but not in front of the needles.

ORDER OF THREADING

Nearly all machines require a certain order for threading, usually upper looper, lower looper, right and then left needle threads. Some machines have a numbered or color-coded diagram (1) inside the looper cover to show the threading order. Always make sure that you thread in the order the manual or machine suggests and take care to go through all the thread guides. Missing a thread guide can result in stitches not forming correctly or threads snapping.

For each of the threads, begin by passing the thread from the spool, through the thread guide on the thread guide bar, and down toward the tension dials (2). There may be an additional thread guide to go through before you get to the tension dial. Pass the thread through the tension dial. Pull on the thread above and below the dial (or on either side of the dial) to ensure that the thread has passed through correctly. Once in place, there should be some resistance on the thread as it is pulled. Leave threads here—each one is explained in more detail in this article below and over the page. Open the side and looper covers (if you have these) to give you better access to the thread guides.

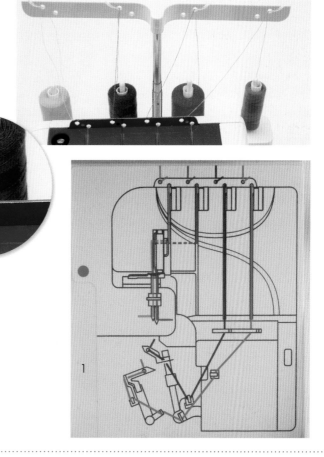

2 From the tension dial, pass the thread through the guides as the manual or machine directs until you get to the eye of the looper. Double-check that you have gone through each guide.

3 Take the thread through the eye of the looper. You may wish to use tweezers or a looper threader to help.

4 Take the thread from the looper, under the presser foot to the back of the machine.

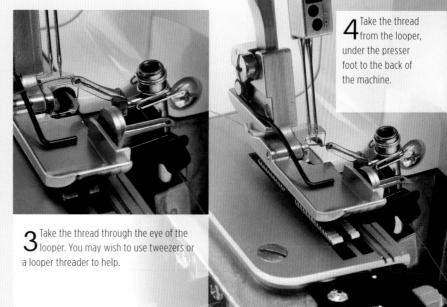

THREADING THE LOWER LOOPER

This is the most difficult to thread, as it has hard-to-reach thread guides. Some brands have made threading of the lower looper easier, so check your manual. Make sure that the lower looper thread sits on top of the upper looper thread and that they do not cross. This can result in snapped threads and having to rethread the machine.

1 Take the thread from the tension dial through the guides as directed on the machine or color-coded diagram until you get to the bottom of the machine. Next, take the threads through the guides leading toward the lower looper.

2 Use your tweezers or looper threader to pass the thread from the right-side opening through to the side opening on the left. Wind the handwheel so that the lower looper appears in the left opening. Pass the thread through the guide at the base and/or top of the left side of the looper, and then use the tweezers to pass the thread from the left-side opening back to the right opening.

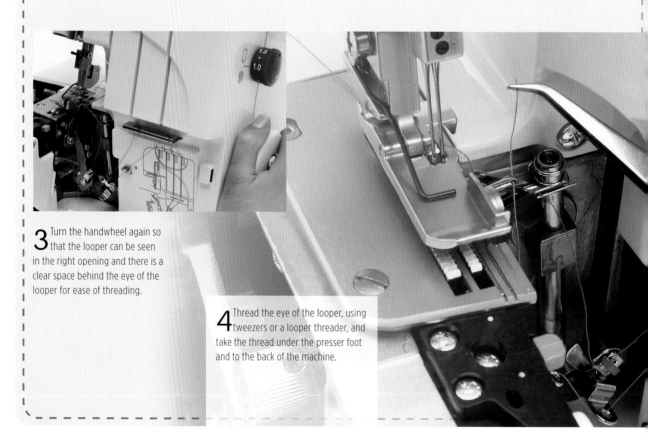

3 Turn the handwheel again so that the looper can be seen in the right opening and there is a clear space behind the eye of the looper for ease of threading.

4 Thread the eye of the looper, using tweezers or a looper threader, and take the thread under the presser foot and to the back of the machine.

Threading the needles

To thread the needles start, first with the right needle. Follow the thread guides from the tension dials as shown on the machine or on the diagrams in the manual, passing finally behind the needle thread guide and then from front to back through the eye of the needle. Use a needle threader to help if you can't see to do this very well, or use tweezers to pull the thread out the back of the needle.

Thread the left needle in the same way. Take the needle threads under the presser foot and toward the back of the machine.

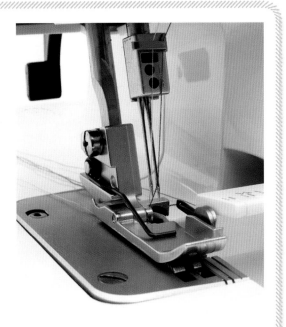

A needle threader can make life a little easier.

Tip
If you find threading tricky, remove the presser foot, releasing it using the lever at the back. With the foot out of the way, you have more room for your fingers to thread the needles.

Before you start to serge

• Make sure that the thread guide bar is pulled up into its highest position.
• All threads should be going through the tension dials and thread guides correctly.
• The lower looper thread must be on top of the upper looper thread.
• The needle threads must be free from the loopers and passing only under the presser foot.
• All threads should be seen on the top of the needle plate, going under the presser foot to the back of the machine.
• Make sure that the machine is plugged in and switched on.

Pull the thread guide bar to its highest position.

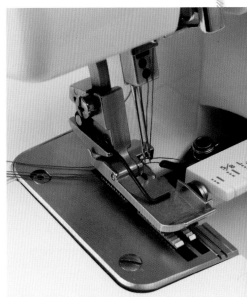

Threads should go under the presser foot and be visible on top of the needle plate.

CHANGING THE THREADS

Once your machine is threaded, keep an eye out for the spools running low—changing the spools before the thread runs out completely can save you a lot of time.

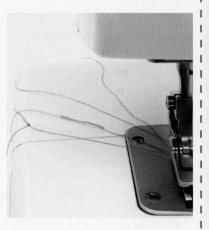

1 To change a spool of thread because it has run down or you want to change the thread color, don't unthread the machine! Cut the threads near to the spool and tie the new threads onto these. The new threads can then be pulled through the machine without the need to get out the looper threader or tweezers. This will save you lots of time!

2 Pull each thread through the machine one at a time so as not to break the threads. Carefully pull the threads through the tension dials—you may need to release tension completely or pull the knots out and over the tension dials and then reposition the new thread into the tension dial. Pulling the knots through the tension controls can damage this part of the machine.

3 Once the threads are through the tension dials, pull them from the needle plate toward the back of the machine, making sure the knots don't get caught in the thread guides. The knots should be small enough to pass through the eyes of the loopers. With thicker threads you may need to use a looper threader or tweezers. For the needle threads pull the new threads through the thread guides, making sure that the knots don't get stuck. Once the knots reach the eye of the needle, you will have to cut the thread and rethread the needles.

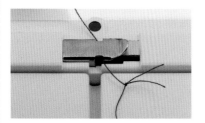

Guide knots through "clip"-type thread guides.

Run all threads under the presser foot.

Use tweezers to pull the needle threads from under the loopers.

Keep your machine clean and lint free.

Tips

• If your machine has "clip"-type thread guides, you may need to help the knots through these clips when changing the threads to avoid any snapping threads.

• Make sure all threads run under the presser foot and toward the back of the machine.

• If upper or lower loopers need to be rethreaded, always use tweezers to pull the needle threads from under the loopers and needle plate and pass them under the presser foot and to the back of the machine. Make sure the threads are not caught up or wrapped around the lower looper. If this is not done, you may find that the thread keeps breaking and you can't work out why.

• Sergers are much easier to thread if the machine is clean and lint free—make sure you keep on top of cleaning your machine.

Getting comfortable

Your machine is threaded and you're ready to have a go. But before you start, make sure you will be comfortable. A good posture is really important, especially if you will be sewing for some time; the wrong position could leave you with back and shoulder aches. Sewing is meant to be relaxing and enjoyable—not something that causes you pain and injury!

WORKING SURFACE

Choosing the right space to sew is important. If you are working on a small table or desk, position your machine in the middle. If you have a large table, sit the machine slightly to the right. Having space to the left of your machine to support the weight of your fabric is important, especially when working with bulky or large items, such as curtains or tablecloths. If you don't have something beneath the fabric it can drag toward the floor, pulling on the needles of the machine and making it harder for you to sew. Some machines come with an extension table to increase your sewing surface; for other sergers you can purchase one as an additional accessory. If you don't have room on your table for all of the fabric in your project, try using a chair or stool to the left of your machine to support the end of the fabric that you're not stitching.

Tips
• Make sure your power cord is not too tight. Use an extension cord if necessary.
• Position the serger near the edge of a desk or table and your foot pedal on the floor so that you can reach it easily with your dominant foot.
• Turn the foot pedal so that the narrowest part is toward you—this will give you better control of the foot and the speed at which you operate the machine.
• Don't expect to be able to watch TV as you sew—opt for the radio or play some music. You do need to pay attention while sewing and keep your eye on the needles and knife blade at all times!

CHAIR HEIGHT

Use a chair that allows you to sit comfortably at the table without having to reach up to your machine or hunch over it. Think about a position you might adopt if you were working at a computer keyboard—being too high or too low in your seat can really cause problems for your wrists and shoulders.

USING THE FOOT PEDAL

All sergers come with a foot pedal, and generally these all look the same. If you're used to using one for controlling the speed of your sewing machine, then you'll get to grips with the serger foot pedal quickly. Be prepared though—it might take some getting used to and may initially sew more quickly than anticipated! This can be a bit scary for beginners, who can find that the serger runs away with them, making them feel out of control. Don't worry—after a little practice with the serger, you'll feel much more confident.

Some foot pedals have a speed setting that allows you to set it to high or low speed. For some decorative techniques it is best to sew slowly to ensure that all of the stitches are being formed correctly, whereas for most serging of seam allowances you'll want to sew quickly, cutting and edge finishing your fabrics with ease and speed. Take your time to begin with until you feel happy about controlling the speed and edge of the fabric or seams.

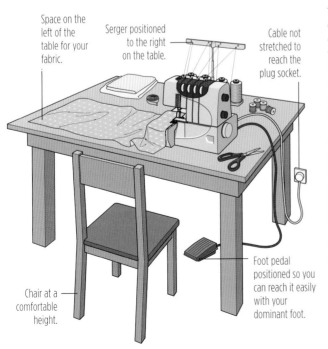

Space on the left of the table for your fabric.

Serger positioned to the right on the table.

Cable not stretched to reach the plug socket.

Foot pedal positioned so you can reach it easily with your dominant foot.

Chair at a comfortable height.

Getting started

Now that you're in the correct position you can begin serging, but first do it without any fabric—yes, you can do this! On a conventional sewing machine this is a bad idea, but on the serger this is perfectly normal and helps you to see that the stitches are forming correctly.

Testing the serger

1 You'll need to have long enough threads coming from the needles and loopers to be able to take hold of them—around 4–6in (10–15cm). Pull the threads gently under the presser foot and to the left.

2 To make sure that the stitches are forming correctly on the stitch finger, turn the handwheel toward you with your right hand while holding the threads gently in your left hand.

3 Pull the threads gently behind the needle under the presser foot and to the left. If the stitching looks correct, lower your foot onto the pedal and sew for a short time so that a tail of serging comes out of the machine—around 2–3in (4–6cm) is ideal.

4 The stitches should look like this. If the stitch doesn't look right, or your threads snap, then look through the checklist on page 37.

SERGING YOUR FIRST PIECE OF FABRIC

When the machine is sewing a chain of serging smoothly and evenly, it's time to try it out on some fabrics. Use a medium-weight cotton fabric, as this will be the easiest to work with as you get to grips with your machine.

And remember, when you are working on a project, always test sew first, using scraps of the fabric you are working with or other scraps in the same weight as your project. The tension dials may need adjusting for different fabrics, so it's best to use a similar or the same one for your trial runs.

As the fabric goes into the machine, aim to cut off just a small amount of the edge with the knife. As the fabric comes out the back, watch as the machine serges the edge neatly. A single piece of fabric around 8in (20cm) in length is ideal to get you started.

Tip
Factory tests and servicing or oiling your machine may leave behind excess oil. To remove this, always sew first onto some scrap fabrics before you try out stitches on your projects.

2 Line up the raw edge on the right-hand side with the edge of the cover. You should be able to see the knife. Try to position the fabric so that the knife will trim off a small amount of fabric from the right-hand side.

1 Begin with the bulk of the fabric to the left of the needle. Push the top edge of the fabric up to the presser foot. You don't need to raise the foot to begin sewing unless you are using heavyweight fabric.

3 Sew slowly; the fabric will automatically feed under the presser foot and out the back. Position your hands at the top edge of the fabric, feeding the fabric under the presser foot. Keep your fingers away from the blade! You don't need to give the fabric much guidance, as the feed dog teeth will do their job of feeding the fabric through the machine. If you try to pull at the fabric at the front or back of the machine you could end up causing some damage, so be gentle and patient.

4 Watch as the knife trims the edge of the fabric as it is fed under the foot. As the fabric comes out the back, it will be neatly serged along the edge.

5 Once the entire length has been fed through the machine keep sewing, creating a chain of serging at the back of the machine. Sew until this thread chain can be cut using the thread cutter on the left of the machine (or behind the needle). Admire your first piece of serging!

Tips
• When you use the serger you don't usually need to raise or lower the presser foot, as the fabric will be automatically fed under the foot and toward the needles. For heavy or slippery fabrics, you may need to lift the foot and position the fabric just before the knife blade to ensure that the feed dog teeth can grip and feed the fabrics through the machine.
• Leave a 4-in (10-cm) thread chain each time you sew. If you cut this chain shorter, you can end up losing the end of the threads and having to rethread the machine.
• If your serged edge doesn't look like the one in the picture at the top left of this page, take a look at the checklist on page 37 or at pages 34–43 for details of how to adjust your machine settings.

Fixing mistakes

**As with all sewing, at some point you may go wrong. Don't worry—
it happens to everyone. In most cases, there will be a number of
remedies that you can try to put things right, cutting off the stitching
to remove the mistake, arming yourself with a quick unpicker to
remove the stitches, or just restarting above the mistake.**

SORTING OUT PROBLEMS

If your serging starts to go wrong, or your machine malfunctions with
snapping threads or clogging stitches, pull the fabric out to the left and,
if you can, continue to stitch, creating a thread chain. If you can't
continue to sew, stop, turn the flywheel toward you to remove the
needle from the fabric, and loosen the tensions on the dials. Pull the
fabric to the left, pulling on the threads if they need a bit of easing out.
Cut the thread and then look for the cause of the mistake. Always stitch
on fabric scraps to make sure that the machine is stitching correctly
before starting again on your project fabric.

REMOVING STITCHES

For more obvious errors on the edging of fabric, or for seams that really
do need removing, you will need to pull out or unpick the stitches and
start again. This may seem complicated and can be a little fussy, but
done in the correct way the threads can be removed easily.

There are a number of techniques for removing stitches, three of
which are described below and at right. Some are quick and some a bit
more time consuming, depending on the fabric and threads you are
working with.

Restarting
If you have used a sewing
machine to make your seam
and are using the serger for
finishing the raw edges, you
may have enough seam
allowance left to cut off the
incorrect serging stitches with
your machine and make a new
edge to the fabric.

In some cases, you may want
to just restart from where the
mistake was made. Lift the
presser foot and reposition the
fabric under the foot with the
needles just above where the
mistake was made. Start
sewing again and continue
along to the end of the seam.

SIMPLY PULL THE THREADS OUT
This method works on shorter seams,
general-purpose threads, and light- to
mediumweight fabrics.

1 If you have a thread chain, straighten this out
with your fingers. The threads for the loopers
will be longer than the needle threads, so try to
separate the needle threads. Gently pull on the
needle threads; the fabric will gather up as you do
this. Continue to pull the needle threads, easing
out the fabric. The threads should eventually pull
out of the fabric completely.

2 Now that the looper threads are no longer
held in place by the needle threads, they
should begin to ravel and can be pulled away
from the fabric.

3 Resew the seam, making sure that the
needles go into the fabric in the same place
as before—in most cases, you don't want to cut
off any more fabric with the knife blade; only
remove any strands of fibers that have begun
to fray.

UNPICKING STITCHES—QUICK METHOD

For some heavier fabrics and also for longer seams or edge finishing, you may need tools to remove the stitches.

1 Snip with small scissors or use an unpicker to break the needle threads only at intervals along the serging stitches. Pull out the needle threads in sections.

2 The looper threads will begin to ravel, making them easier to pull away from the fabric.

3 Resew the seam, making sure that the needles go into the fabric in the same place as before—in most cases, you don't want to cut off any more fabric with the knife blade; only remove any strands of fibers that have begun to fray.

UNPICKING STITCHES—LONGER METHOD

When either pulling the threads out (left) or the quick unpick method (above) don't work, try removing the threads by pulling the seam apart and running your unpicker along the threads. This is the technique you would use for unpicking a seam made on a normal sewing machine. For 4-thread stitching where you have used both left and right needles, this can be a time-consuming job.

Alternatively, run the unpicker along the edge of the serging, cutting through the looper threads. These can then be removed and the needle threads pulled out. This often results in many short threads needing to be pulled out and it can be a very slow process making sure that all threads are removed.

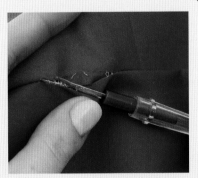

Pull the seam apart and run the unpicker along the threads.

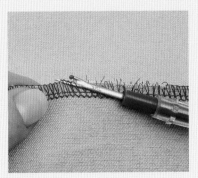

Run the unpicker along a serged edge to cut looper threads, which will then need to be removed.

HOLES IN THE FABRIC

At some point every sewer will make this mistake. Take your eyes off the blade for a moment and you realize you have cut into the fabric where you didn't really want to.

Small nicks

For a quick fix, try ironing some fusible interfacing onto the wrong side of the fabric—this doesn't work for every hole you make, but can patch up small, inconspicuous nicks into fabric.

Large holes

For larger holes, depending on the position of the hole, you may need to start again.

Tip

Tweezers with fine tips usually come as an accessory with your machine. They are great for picking up threads on delicate fabrics, as they don't have a point or cutting edge. They are also ideal for removing basting stitches that are close to the serge stitching.

Finishing and securing ends

How can you stop the threads from raveling? Unlike the sewing machine, the serger has no reverse lever to cover over and secure the start and end of the sewing. In most cases you do not need to do anything to secure the start and end of a seam, but if the seam will not be covered by further stitching, or if it is in an obvious place, you may need to secure the end.

> **Tip**
> Some machines have a back baste device to secure the threads at the start of a seam or edging. When the threads are pulled to the front (see step 2, below), secure them under the back baste device before continuing to sew.

PREVENT THREADS FROM RAVELING

Listed below are five options for how you can prevent threads from raveling. As with other sewing techniques, choose the method that will be best for your fabric or project.

Do nothing

On some garments you will often sew a seam over the end of another serged seam, making it secure. When making a skirt with a waistband and machined hem, for example, the seams are sewn and serged first, and then the waistband is stitched across the top of the side seams. This means that you do not need to worry about securing them. The hem will then be turned up and sewn across the other ends of the side seams.

Cut and pull the remaining threads tight

Pull on the threads to draw them in toward each other and cut, leaving a short end—1/4in (5mm) or less. Pull the threads again to further secure.

Use a seam sealant

There are a variety of these available from sewing shops or notions departments. Use the smallest of drops on the end of the seam to secure the threads. Once the sealant is dry, cut the thread chain close to the end of the fabric.

Tie a knot in the thread chain

Tie a knot in the chain and slide it so that it sits next to the end of the seam. Use sealant if desired, or just cut the threads close to the knot.

Weave in the ends

Use a bodkin, loop turner, crochet hook, or large-eyed needle to pull the chain through the stitches of the seam. Cut the long ends close to the seam.

TAIL END AT THE START OF A SEAM
This technique can be used at the start of the seam. Although it takes a bit more time than some of the other methods, it makes a neat and secure finish.

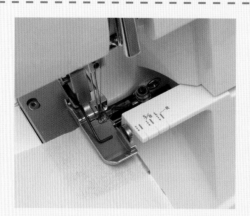

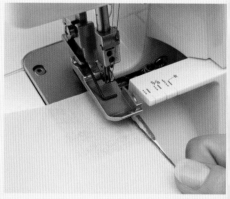

1 Stitch along the seam line for two to three stitches only. Turn the handwheel toward you until the needle is inserted into the fabric. (Some machines may have an automatic "needle down" button.)

2 Lift the presser foot. Bring the thread chain from the back of the fabric to the front and under the presser foot. Don't pull too tight—the fabric should remain flat at the start of the seam. Lower the presser foot.

TAIL END AT THE END OF A SEAM

This can be a bit of a fussy technique, depending on how easily the threads can be removed from the stitch finger. Once mastered, it gives a neat and secure finish to the end of the seam.

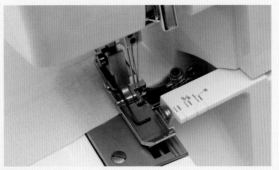

1 Stitch to the end of the seam until the needle stitches just off the fabric. Turn the flywheel toward you until the needle is out of the fabric and in its highest position.

2 Raise the presser foot and remove the threads from the stitch finger.

3 Flip the fabric toward you so that the serged edge goes back under the foot, ready for you to sew back over it. Stitch along the edge for $1\frac{1}{8}$–$1\frac{1}{2}$in (3–4cm) at a slight angle so as not to cut off any of the original threads. Pull the fabric out to the left, leaving a chain of serged thread, before cutting close the edge of the fabric.

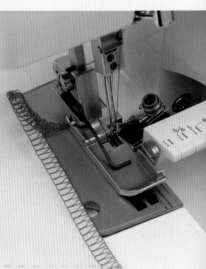

3 Continue to stitch forward, enclosing the thread chain in the serged edge. Cut off any excess thread with the serger blade. If the seam has begun to gather in from the start or look puckered, gently flatten out the seam with your fingers.

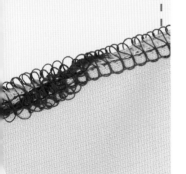

Tips for releasing the threads from the stitch finger

• Pull hard on the fabric at the back of the machine—on some models, this may loosen the threads on the stitch finger. Pull the threads off with your fingers.
• Pull on the needle threads just above the last thread guide before the needle—this will help ease the tension on the threads over the stitch finger.
• If your machine can be adjusted for rolled hemming by removing the stitch finger with a sliding knob or lever, you may be able to use this to wiggle the stitch finger and loosen the threads.

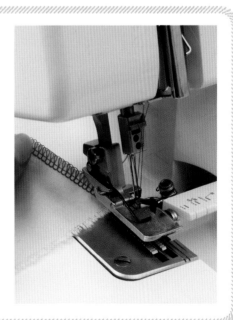

Adjusting the serger settings

Your serger will come with a number of adjustable settings to help you create the perfect finish for any fabric. You need to know how each one works and how they can be adjusted to create the perfect serged stitch.

ADJUSTABLE SETTINGS

There are six general setting changes that you can make on your machine to adjust the appearance of the stitches that your serger will produce.

These are:
❶ Cutting width
❷ Thread tensions
❸ Stitch length
❹ Stitch width
❺ Differential feed
❻ Foot pressure

Altering any one of these will have a certain effect on the outcome of your serged stitches. They will be discussed in more detail over the following nine pages.

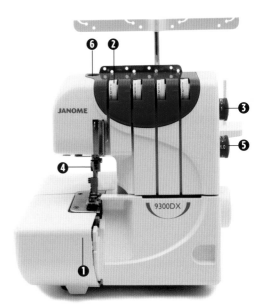

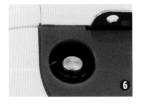

Shall I adjust my settings?

Always sew a test seam and check your stitching. Build up an assortment of fabrics to use for practice stitching. Always use a fabric in the same or similar weight to your project material to ensure the correct balance of tensions. Does your stitching:

• Hold securely without the seam pulling apart? (1)
• Look correct without any thread loops or strained stitches? (2)
• Sit flat without puckering? (3)
• Not stretch the fabric at the serged edge? (4)
• Suit your fabric, not appearing too bulky or too fine? (5)

If you can't answer "yes" to all the above, then you need to adjust your machine settings. There may be more than one adjustment necessary to correct your stitching.

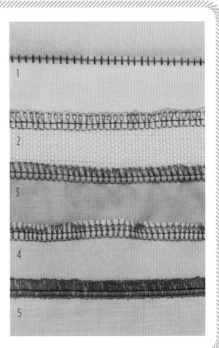

Adjusting the cutting width

The cutting width is the distance from the left needle to the cutting blade or the width of fabric within the serged loops. It can be controlled with a dial that adjusts the lower knife position. The upper knife will automatically line up with the new lower knife position.

Cutting width dial on Janome 9300DX

KNIFE BLADE

Nearly all machines have a retractable knife blade, allowing you to move the knife blade out of the way completely, disengaging it to create edge finishes without cutting any fabric away. On some models, the serger blade can also be moved to the left or right to adjust the cutting width of the machine. Adjustments made are only tiny, but can affect the stitching of the machine. Adjusting the cutting width needs to be done in conjunction with adjusting the stitch width. Threads should lie on the edge of the fabric without loops appearing beyond the cut edge or the fabric being slightly rolled inside the enclosed stitch. On more advanced machines where a number of stitches can be selected, the machine will automatically set the cutting width for specific stitch effects. On more basic machines, the blade is moved manually using a dial or lever. Instructions with the machine will give guidance on the setting to use. Check your manual to see if your machine has this setting and where to find it.

Your machine will have a neutral or preferable setting, sometimes marked on the dial or described in the manual. The dial will be numbered or have "+/-" on it. Move the dial to a larger number to increase cutting width or turn toward "+." Turn the dial toward a lower number or toward "-" to decrease the cutting width.

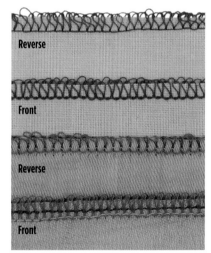

Cutting width dial on Janome 1200D

Balancing the cutting width and stitch width settings

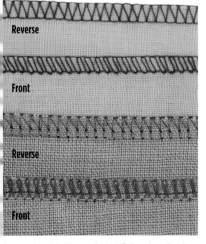

Reverse

Front

Reverse

Front

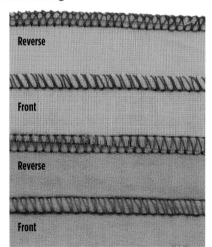

Reverse

Front

Reverse

Front

Reverse

Front

Reverse

Front

A balanced stitch. Here we look at 3-thread serging (top examples) and 4-thread serging (bottom examples).

The cutting width has been set too wide for the stitch width. The fabric is rolled within the stitch and doesn't sit flat. Adjust the stitch width to make it wider or adjust the cutting width to make this narrower.

The cutting width has been set too narrow and doesn't suit the stitch width. Thread loops appear beyond the cut edge. Adjust the stitch width to make this narrower or make the cutting width wider.

Adjusting the thread tensions

All serger models have adjustable tension dials or knobs on the front or top of the machine. These control how tightly or loosely the thread is held and pulled through the machine to ensure that the stitches are always correctly balanced. Some mid- to high-range sergers have automatic tension setting on the dials, so the machine sets itself to the most suitable tension setting for different stitches. Thread tensions can be fine-tuned to adjust these settings further if the stitch produced does not look quite right.

TENSION DIAL POSITION

In most cases, the machine will work a balanced stitch for mediumweight fabrics and general-purpose serger threads, with all the tension dials set to the neutral position. (Check your manual to see what this is.) For heavier or lighter fabrics and for different threads, you may need to adjust the dials to create the perfect stitch.

As a general rule, the thicker the thread the looser the tension dial will need to be. On the tension dials you will find either a numbered system or "+/–" markings on or next to the dials. The higher the number or the more you turn toward the "+" on the dial, the higher the tension or the tighter the thread is held in the machine. Conversely, the lower the number or the further you turn toward the "–" on the dial, the looser the thread will be held and pulled through the machine. Because even the same model of machine may need the tension dials adjusting in different ways, this information should just serve as guidance to setting up your machine correctly.

Here the serger has been rethreaded with different-colored threads to match the color coding in the looper cover, so that you can really see the

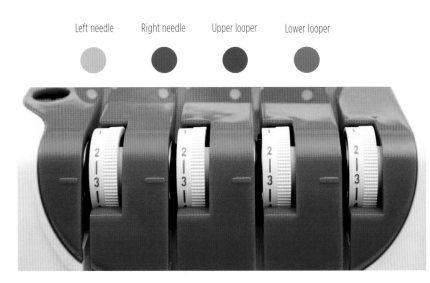

Left needle   Right needle   Upper looper   Lower looper

In the examples on pages 37–39, different-colored threads have been used for the two needles and two loopers as shown above, so you can see the effect of adjusting each tension dial.

difference in the thread tensions. Try this on your own machine, using the "cut, knot, and pull through" method of rethreading. This will help you to see more clearly which thread is out of tension and needs adjusting. Try adjusting the tension to see what effects this will have on your stitching.

The adjustments at right will give you some guidance on adjusting your tension dials for common balance issues. Work through the checklist at right before you start adjusting your tension settings. If you do need to adjust the tension, change

only one thread at a time. Start with the thread that looks the most out of place. Stitch, check, and adjust again if necessary until the desired stitch is produced. If changing the tension doesn't help and you are still having problems, it may be the cutting width that needs changing or something else has gone awry (see Adjusting the cutting width, page 35).

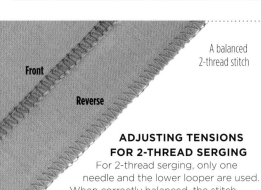

A balanced
2-thread stitch

ADJUSTING TENSIONS FOR 2-THREAD SERGING

For 2-thread serging, only one needle and the lower looper are used. When correctly balanced, the stitch should look like the picture above.

LEFT OR RIGHT NEEDLE THREAD

As you stitch with only two threads, the needle thread should appear as a straight stitch on the top side of the fabric and lie flat in a V-shape on the under side. Tension dials may need to be tightened or loosened to achieve the correct appearance. If the needle thread is too loose, the thread will be pulled to the top side over the edge of the fabric. If the needle thread is too tight, the looper threads will be pulled round to the under side of the fabric.

LOWER LOOPER THREAD

This should lie flat on the top side of the fabric and appear only on the fabric edge on the underside, locking with the needle thread. You may need to loosen the needle thread and then tighten the looper thread, or vice versa, to achieve the correct result. Only adjust one at a time, sew for a short while, and then inspect the stitch. Alter, and sew again, repeating this until you are happy with the stitch produced.

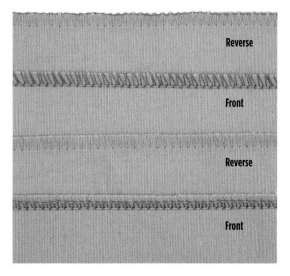

Needle tension too loose (top examples) and needle tension too tight (bottom examples).

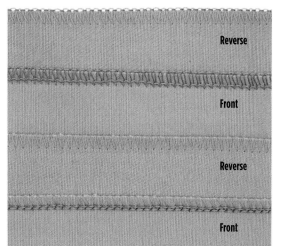

Looper tension too loose (top examples) and looper tension too tight (bottom examples).

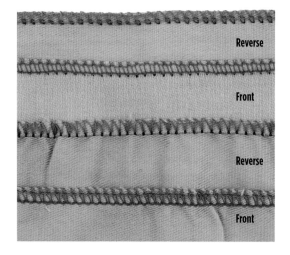

A balanced 3-thread stitch

ADJUSTING TENSIONS FOR 3-THREAD SERGING

For the correct tension on the threads, the stitch should look like the picture above.

The needle thread will appear as a straight row of stitching on the top side of the fabric and as a loop wrapped around the lower looper threads on the under side of the fabric. The upper looper thread will appear as for the 4-thread stitch, sitting on the top side of the fabric, appearing just on the edge of the under side of the fabric. The lower looper thread will appear just on the edge of the top side of the fabric and across the underside of the fabric.

Needle tension too loose (top examples) and needle tension too tight (bottom examples).

LEFT OR RIGHT NEEDLE THREAD

Only one needle is used for 3-thread serging, so making sure that the tension on this one needle thread is correct is really important. If 3-thread serging is being used to create a seam, then this row of stitching must be balanced correctly to avoid the seam pulling apart. Just as with 4-thread serging, a stitch that is too loose will pull apart at the seam, whereas a stitch that is too tight will result in a puckered seam and runs the risk of breaking.

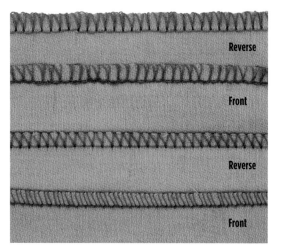

Lower looper tension too loose (top examples) and lower looper tension too tight (bottom examples).

LOWER LOOPER THREAD

This thread should be seen on the wrong side of the fabric and only just be visible on the upper side of the fabric, sitting just on the edge of the fabric. A thread that is too loose will be pulled around to the upper side of the fabric. A thread that is too tight will pull the upper looper threads round to the underside of the fabric.

UPPER LOOPER THREAD

This thread should be seen on the right side of the fabric; from the underside of the fabric, the thread will sit just on the edge. A thread that is too loose will be pulled to the underside of the fabric and a thread that is too tight will pull the lower looper thread round to the top side of the fabric.

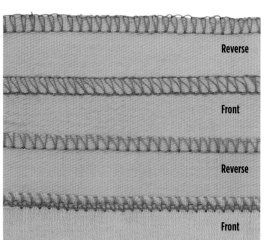

Upper looper tension too loose (top examples) and upper looper tension too tight (bottom examples).

Tip

When balancing the upper and lower loopers, you may need to tighten the upper looper and loosen the lower looper for the stitches to look correct—remember to change only one tension dial at a time.

Front

Reverse

A balanced 4-thread stitch

ADJUSTING TENSIONS FOR 4-THREAD SERGING

For the correct tension on the threads, the stitch should look like the picture above. The needle threads will appear on the upper side of the fabric as two rows of straight stitching over the upper looper threads—the same as a straight stitch produced on a regular sewing machine. On the underside, the needle threads appear as small loops wrapped around the looper threads. The upper looper threads should only appear on the top side of the fabric and the lower looper threads on the underside.

LEFT NEEDLE THREAD

If you are using a serger only to produce a seam, then it's crucial that the left needle thread is at the correct tension. A stitch that is too loose will pull apart at the seam, whereas a stitch that is too tight will result in a puckered seam and runs the risk of breaking.

RIGHT NEEDLE THREAD

This thread acts as a safety thread when stitching with four threads. If it is too loose or too tight it's not too much of a problem, as this thread won't be taking the strain of the seam. However, as far as possible, tension should be altered and adjusted, otherwise the stitch will look wrong.

LOWER LOOPER THREAD

This thread should be seen on the wrong side of the fabric and only just be visible on the upper side of the fabric, sitting on the edge of the fabric. A thread that is too loose will be pulled around to the upper side of the fabric. A thread that is too tight will pull the upper looper threads round to the underside of the fabric.

UPPER LOOPER THREAD

This thread should be seen on the right side of the fabric; from the under side of the fabric, the thread will sit just on the edge. A thread that is too loose will be pulled to the underside of the fabric and a thread that is too tight will pull the lower looper thread round to the top side of the fabric.

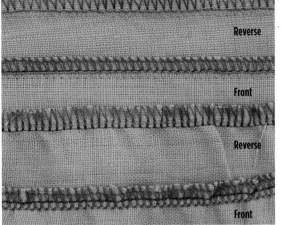

Reverse

Front

Reverse

Front

Left needle tension too loose (top examples) and left needle tension too tight (bottom examples).

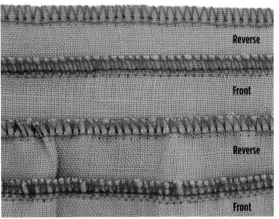

Reverse

Front

Reverse

Front

Right needle tension too loose (top examples) and right needle tension too tight (bottom examples).

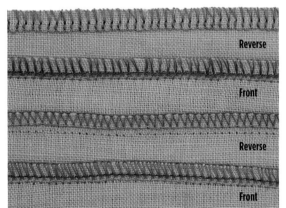

Reverse

Front

Reverse

Front

Lower looper tension too loose (top examples) and lower looper tension too tight (bottom examples).

Reverse

Front

Reverse

Front

Upper looper tension too loose (top examples) and upper looper tension too tight (bottom examples).

Adjusting the stitch length

Nearly all serger machines have a control for stitch length. The range of stitch length available depends on the model of the machine. Generally this varies from 1/64–1/8in (0.5–4mm), although some machines can produce shorter and longer stitches.

STITCH LENGTH CONTROL

The location of the stitch length control differs from model to model. In most cases, a stitch length dial can be found on the right-hand side of the machine, but on some models it may be on the front, left side, or inside one of the looper covers. Check your manual to find where your control is. The dial may be numbered or have "+/-" on it. Just like the stitch length dial on a sewing machine, the larger the number, the longer the stitch. Some dials may also show "R," which would be used for rolled or narrow hem settings (see page 68).

Changing the stitch length is much less daunting than altering any of the other controls. It can easily be moved back to its original position if the resulting stitch is not as desired. The normal setting for stitch length may be marked on the dial as a colored bar or line. Generally, stitch length for normal sewing or mediumweight fabrics is 1/16in (2.5mm). The use of different threads will mean that you may need to alter the stitch length, especially when using bulky decorative threads.

Tips
- For heavier fabrics or threads, use a longer stitch length. For lighter fabrics or threads, use a shorter stitch length. Chiffon, although fine, will need a slightly longer stitch, otherwise the needle can damage or cause pulls on the fabric.
- Always do a test first to check that the stitch length looks right on your fabric.

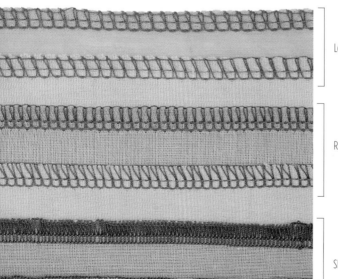

Long stitch length

Regular stitch length

Short stitch length

TENSION

Changing the stitch length can mean that you also need to alter the tension on the machine, especially if the stitch is really short or very long. Shorter stitches may need more tension (higher number) on the needle and looper threads to allow less thread to pass through the machine for each stitch. A longer stitch will most likely need less tension (smaller number) on the needle and looper threads, as more thread is needed to create each stitch and this allows the threads to pass through the machine more easily.

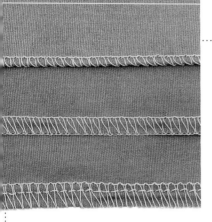

Narrow 3-thread roll hemming

Narrow 3-thread serging

Wide 4-thread serging

ADJUSTING THE STITCH WIDTH

Although there is not always a special dial to alter stitch width, most machines will allow you to control the stitch width in at least one way. More advanced machines will have separate dials, or will automatically change the stitch width for different stitch settings. The range of stitch widths available will depend on the model and can be from 1/16–3in (1.5–7.5mm). For more delicate lightweight fabrics, a narrow stitch width is more desirable; for heavier fabrics, especially loosely woven fabrics, a wider stitch width will secure the edge of the fabric better.

For machines that don't have stitch width dials, using one or other of the needles is the simplest method for adjusting the width of the stitch. For the widest stitch, use the needle on the left, either in addition to the right needle for 4-thread stitching or on its own for 2- or 3-thread stitching. For a narrower stitch, use just the needle on the right, making the gap between the cutting blade and needle smaller.

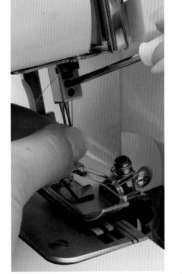

Remove the left needle when you are using only the right needle, or vice versa, to avoid stitching problems.

ADJUSTING THE STITCH FINGER

On some machines the stitch finger can be removed, or moved out of position, to enable narrow or rolled hemming. This will result in a narrower, much finer serging stitch. Check to see if your machine has this feature.

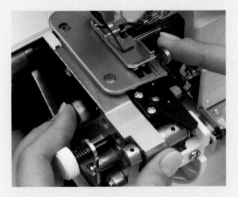

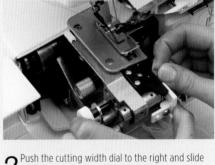

1 Turn off the machine before changing the settings. Open the looper cover and side cover. Push in the knob on the left and rotate to move the knife blade out of the way.

2 Push the cutting width dial to the right and slide the needle plate setting knob from "S" for standard serging to "R" for rolled hemming setting. This will move the stitch finger out of the way. Push in the knob on the left again and rotate to activate the knife. Close the covers.

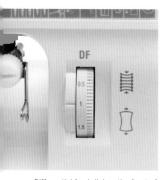

Differential feed dial on the front of the Janome 1200D

Differential feed dial on the side of the Janome 9300DX

Foot pressure adjusting screw on the Janome 9300DX

Foot pressure dial on the top of the Janome 1200D

Adjusting the differential feed

A differential feed isn't available on all machines, but it is really helpful for getting the best finish on different fabrics. Differential feed dials work in conjunction with the feed dog teeth. On a serger, there are two sets of feed dog teeth—one at the front and one at the back. The teeth at the front feed the fabric into the machine, moving it toward and under the foot. The teeth at the back move the fabric out of the machine.

SETTING THE DIAL

Changing the differential feed will allow more or less fabric to be fed into the machine, or more or less fabric to be fed out of the machine. It can be used to eliminate unwanted gathering, stretching, or puckering on seams and hems. It can also be used to create gathers and stretch where required. If the differential feed is set incorrectly, the serged edge can appear stretched and ruffled or may appear gathered. You can use the differential feed dial purposely to achieve these results—for example, to create a lettuce leaf edging for ruffles on a dress, skirt, or tablecloth. Check your manual to find out where your differential feed dial is.

The numbers on the differential feed usually show the ratio of speeds between front and back teeth. All machines have a neutral position where the speed of front and back feed dog teeth is equal—in this case, 1.0. A higher number would indicate the front teeth moving more quickly than the back teeth, which would create a gathered effect on the fabric. Conversely, a lower number on the differential feed dial would indicate the front teeth moving more slowly than the back, creating stretching at the edge of the fabric. Adjustments to the differential feed will have more dramatic results on lightweight fabrics.

ADJUSTING FOOT PRESSURE

For mediumweight fabric, there will usually be no need to adjust the foot pressure. Heavier fabrics can move more easily and evenly through the machine if the foot applies less pressure, whereas for lightweight fabrics more pressure may be needed to get a flatter, unpuckered result. Not all machines have this feature, but it may be used instead of, or as well as, the differential feed dial to control the amount of stretch or gathering given to the edge of fabric as it feeds through the machine.

The foot pressure dial is usually quite small and can be found on the top of the machine above the foot. It will probably have "+" or "–" on the dial.

If your fabric appears stretched as it comes out of the serger, try changing the pressure applied by the foot. Turn the dial toward "–" or toward a lower number so that less pressure is applied by the foot. Turn the dial slightly, sew, and test the setting of your machine. Check the results and then alter the dial again if the seam or hem still appears puckered or stretched.

If your fabric appears gathered as it comes out of the serger, this may be due to not enough pressure being applied by the foot to the fabric. Turn the foot pressure dial toward "+" or toward a higher number to increase the pressure. The result should be an even seam that lies flat without any gathering.

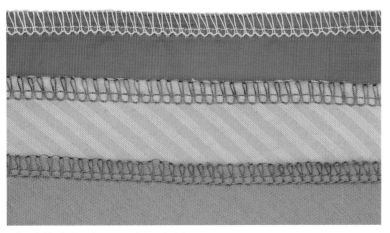

Differential feed adjusted to create a balanced stitch.

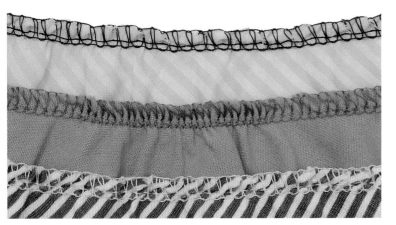

Differential feed set too high, resulting in gathered stitches.

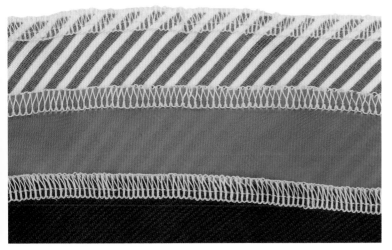

Differential feed set too low, resulting in stretching along the serged edge.

WORKING WITH DIFFERENT FABRICS

Most easy-to-handle fabrics will sew with ease without puckering, stretching, or appearing ruffled. However, some knitted fabrics can be a bit trickier, so you may need to make some adjustments to the settings. Adjusting the differential feed dials will have the most pronounced effect on bias-cut fabrics or on lightweight fabrics such as t-shirt, jersey, or chiffon.

STOPPING FABRIC FROM GATHERING

If your fabric appears gathered, it may be because the differential feed is set too high. The front feed dog teeth are moving too quickly, pushing too much fabric toward the needle, and the rear feed dog teeth are moving too slowly, making the fabric gather along the edge. To adjust this, turn the differential feed dial toward "–" or to a smaller number. The result should be an evenly serged edge. To make the most of the gathered look, turn the differential feed to the highest setting.

STOPPING FABRIC FROM STRETCHING

If the serged edge of your fabric appears stretched or ruffled, this may be because the differential feed is set too low. The fabric is being fed too slowly into the machine and too quickly out of the machine, pulling on the edge of the fabric and making it appear wavy. To remedy this, turn the differential feed dial toward "+" or a larger number. This will allow the front feed dog teeth to move more quickly than the back and stop the fabric from stretching as it is serged.

No differential feed? No problem.

If your machine doesn't have a differential feed setting, use the foot pressure dial instead to allow the machine to work better with different fabrics. Make a slight change to the foot pressure, test, sew, and then check. Alter the pressure again, testing and checking until an even, flat seam or hem is produced.

For lighter fabrics, apply more pressure to the foot; for heavier fabrics, use a lower foot pressure. Check your manual to see if you can adjust the foot pressure.

CHAPTER 2
Techniques

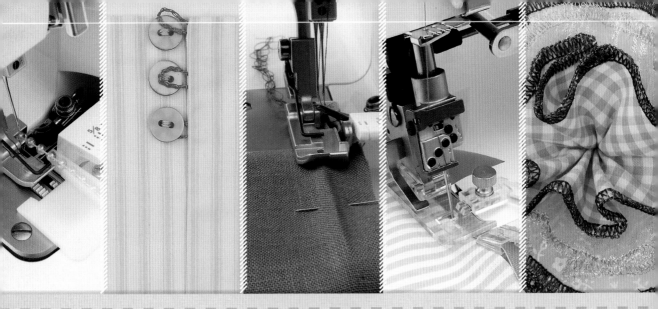

Now you've got to grips with the fundamentals, it's time to learn some techniques. We start at the very beginning, learning where to sew, which stitch to choose, and how to construct a simple seam. From there you'll find a huge range of techniques, from serging circles and curves, to creating mock band hems, and serging with decorative thread. As the chapter progresses further, you will enter the world of feet and attachments, and discover the exciting techniques and finishes that you can achieve with these interesting extras. Each technique includes an Ideas File to provide you with inspiration for decorative and practical applications of the technique.

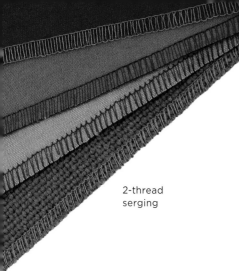

2-thread serging

Basic stitches

The serger is now set up, you've had a little practice to see what the different dials do, and you are ready to serge your first project.

WHICH STITCH DO YOU CHOOSE?
The stitches available to you will depend on the type of serger you have and how many spools the machine can hold and use at one time. Most basic machines will offer 3- or 4-thread serging, whereas some may allow you to work with two or even five threads. This

	MACHINE TYPE	APPROPRIATE TEXTILES	HOW THE STITCH IS FORMED
2-THREAD SERGING	Check your manual to see if this stitch is available to you. Some machines come with a separate "2-thread converter" that is applied to the upper looper and enables the machine to work with just two threads.	• Sheer fabrics or lightweight knits: seams or edge finishing. • Single layers of mediumweight fabrics: edge finishing.	Stitch is created from two threads, one in the needle and one in the lower looper.
3-THREAD SERGING	Available on most machines. Remove one of the needles to create a 3-thread stitch.	Suitable for most fabrics. • Use the narrow setting for sheer and lightweight fabrics or for areas where there will be little stress on the seams. • Use the wider setting for medium- to heavyweight fabrics, as this is more secure.	• Stitch is formed from the threads of one needle and two loopers. • Stitch setting can be altered to be wide or narrow depending on whether the left or right needle position is chosen. • When using three threads only, remove one of the needles to avoid unwanted holes in your fabric or irregular stitching.
4-THREAD SERGING	Available on nearly all machines.	• Ideal for knit or stretch fabrics or on other medium- to heavyweight fabrics, especially where the seams will come under stress. • Works well on loose-weave fabrics where the extra line of straight stitching adds strength to the seams.	Stitch formed from two needles and two loopers.
5-THREAD SERGING	Only available on machines that can hold and use five spools of thread.	Medium- to heavyweight woven fabrics.	5 threads form a secure stitch made up of a chain stitch and a serged stitch. • The chain stitch uses the threads from one needle and the chaining looper. • The 3-thread serging stitch is formed by the other needle and the upper and lower loopers.

section begins by giving you a quick guide to the basic serge stitches available on most machines, before moving on to more advanced stitches, such as roll hemming (pages 68–69) and flatlocking (pages 74–75).

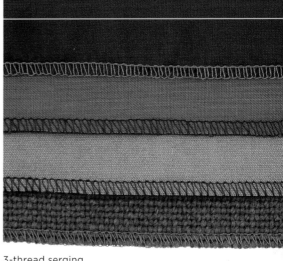

3-thread serging

ADVANTAGES	DISADVANTAGES
Less bulky and stretchier than 3-thread stitches, as there are fewer threads.	The threads meet at the fabric edge and not at the seam line, so the stitch can be pulled apart to lie flat. This is great for flatlocking, but not so good for seams.
• Less bulky than using 4 threads. • Can be set to wide or narrow settings. • Quick to unpick or remove.	Leaving one unused needle in place can sometimes cause irregular stitch patterns or holes in the fabric.
• There are two rows of straight stitching, giving a more secure seam to make projects stronger and more durable. • Still has some stretch.	• More time consuming to unpick or remove. • Uses lots of thread to form stitches.
• Stitch has more durability than the 4-thread serge stitch. • Excellent for seams that will come under a large amount of stress. • More flexibility in the creation of decorative stitches.	• Stitch has little, if any, stretch. • Uses 5 threads, so can become bulky and costly to produce.

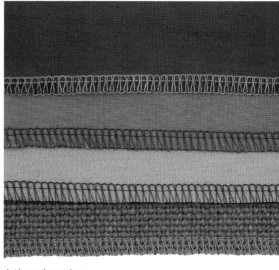

4-thread serging

5-thread serging

Simple seams

Whenever you make anything, you'll need to sew a seam. No matter what type of seam you choose, you must make sure that you've cut your fabric large enough to allow for it. If you don't, you may sew up your project and find that your garment, purse, or pillow is too small. This extra fabric is referred to as the seam allowance on a pattern or fabric piece.

SEAM ALLOWANCE

Dressmaking patterns and other home-sewing projects generally have a seam allowance of ⅝in (1.5cm) along the edges of all the pattern pieces where you need to sew a seam. The instructions that come with your pattern or project will give guidance on which type of seam technique to use and the seam allowance given. Those familiar with using a sewing machine will already have mastered a simple, straight seam to the correct seam allowance. When it comes to achieving a serged seam ⅝in (1.5cm) from the edge of the fabric, it can take a little practice to get your stitches in the right place. Be careful—don't line up your fabric in the wrong place, as the blade might cut too much of it away.

WHERE SHOULD I SEW?

Those new to the serger often ask where to sew or how they can achieve an even seam on their projects. This isn't always easy when you first start. It is really easy to cut off all the seam allowance and stitch too far over. If you're trying to achieve a seam that is ⅝in (1.5cm) from the edge of the fabric, don't position the fabric so that the blade cuts along this line, as you'll end up with a much smaller seam.

If you're making clothes, it is a good idea to sew the seams on your sewing machine first, then try your garment on and adjust. Once you know that the garment fits, use the serger to trim and finish the seam allowance.

Tips
• Sew your seams first on a sewing machine and then serge the seam allowance.
• For fabrics that ravel really easily, serge all the pieces first before sewing them together on your sewing machine.
• When serging a seam stitched with a sewing machine, a good rule of thumb is to cut off the tiniest amount with the blade—just enough to remove any fraying edges. You can always go back and cut more off if you want to make the seam allowance smaller, but you can't add it back on again!
• Use a cloth guide (left) to help keep a straight and even seam.

A cloth guide will ensure an even seam.

Holding pieces together
• Pins can be used to hold seams together, but always remove them as the fabric approaches the needle plate. Never use pins near the blades of the serger. Unlike with a sewing machine, you can't sew over the pins. If you do make this mistake, you'll only do it once—the blade can't cut through metal pins and your machine may break.
• It is possible to sew on the serger without pins. The machine will keep two pieces of fabric together and evenly feed them through without puckering or pulling one layer through more than the other.
• You can use small clothespins, paper clips, or quilt binding clips for really heavy fabrics. These should all be removed from the fabric as they get closer to the presser foot.
• Basting tapes or a water soluble glue will keep the edges of the fabric together when serging, although it's not the best method for all fabrics. Sometimes this method can take longer than machine or hand basting and can make more of a mess! Always do a test run first to see what the finished result looks like and read the instructions carefully.

GETTING YOUR SEAM IN THE RIGHT PLACE

If you want to use the serger only for a quick finish, or are using a fabric that is better suited to serging than to machine sewing (such as jersey and knitted fabrics), there are a few ways to make sure your seam will be in the right place. The following techniques explain different methods of achieving a perfect equally measured seam. You can choose the one that suits you, the way you like to work, and your fabric choice. The more you sew, the easier it gets to judge a $5/8$in (1.5cm) seam line and know where to line up your fabric.

MARKING THE SEAM LINE ONTO THE FABRIC

Tailor's chalk or a vanishing fabric marker can be used to mark the seam line before you feed the fabric through the serger. Alternatively, machine or hand baste the fabric first, using the methods described below and right, to give you a thread line to work from.

Hand basting the seam line

This is an alternative to using machine basting. If you use a thread color that matches your fabric, you can avoid having to unpick and remove the basting thread. This method is great for eliminating the need to use pins when serging but, depending on your hand-sewing skills, you don't always get an even and straight line. Where you would prefer to remove the basting thread after stitching, use a thread color that will stand out. For some fabrics, such as slippery silk, this may be the best way to prepare your fabric for serging.

MACHINE BASTING

Use thread to mark the seam line by machine basting it with your sewing machine. This ensures that you start with the correct seam allowance before you start serging and cutting the edge off. Machine basting can be quicker than drawing the line onto your fabric and is ideal for tricky fabrics such as chiffons or lightweight jersey. You also eliminate the need to use pins when you come to serging, thus avoiding any accidental damage to the knife blade.

1 Use your sewing machine to machine baste a seam $5/8$in (1.5cm) from the edge of the fabric. This can be done by setting your sewing machine to the longest stitch setting and then using the guides on the needle plate to achieve a perfect seam. Use a thread that matches your fabric—this way you can avoid having to remove the basting thread once you have serged.

2 Now serge the seam. The basting line should be positioned in line with the needle on the left. As you serge, the left needle will stitch on the basting line and the blade will cut off the remaining fabric, leaving you with a seam of around $1/4$in (5mm), depending on the stitch width settings for your serger. (See the stitch width section on page 41 for more information.)

3 You must ensure that the seam is stitched on the basting line. The basting stitches are large and don't hold the fabric as closely or as tightly as normal stitching, so you can't just cut off the edge of the seam allowance and keep the basting as your permanent seam. Any noticeable basting threads can be removed once the serging is complete.

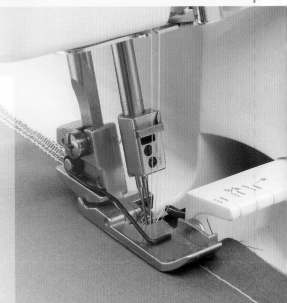

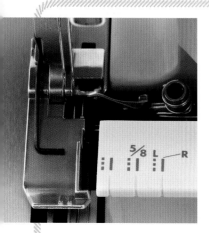

Using the stitching guidelines

On some models, you will find stitching guidelines on the right looper cover. Often these are marked "L" and "R" to show the distance from the left and right needle. If you are trying to sew a seam $5/8$in (1.5cm) from the edge of the fabric, use this to help correctly position your fabric.

If you do use these guidelines, be aware that the seam line will be where the needle forms the stitching on the left, not where the blade cuts the fabric. The blade will then cut off the rest of the fabric, leaving you with a seam of around $1/4$in (5mm).

Using the guidelines on the needle plate of a sewing machine is easy, as the fabric sits flat on the plate of the machine. It's not as easy to use the guidelines on the serger, as the fabric doesn't sit flat and begins to fold out of the way as the blade cuts. When you first start, you may want to try some of these alternative methods.

If you don't have guidelines on your machine, measure from the left needle and use masking tape or a pencil to make your own guidelines.

FINISHING EDGES

The simplest seam is sewn with a straight stitch on the sewing machine. Usually the seam allowance, or raw edge left after the seam has been sewn, is finished afterward to stop the fabric from fraying. This can be done in a number of ways, such as zigzag stitching along the edge or cutting with pinking shears.

With a serger, you can sew the seam and edge finish all in one go. Although this may seem like a quick and easy option, depending on the project it may be best to sew the seam on the sewing machine first and then finish the edge with the serger. If you're making garments you will need to sew seams first and only serge the edge once you have checked the fit is right and made any alterations to the size. Just using the serger can mean you've cut off your seam allowances and now can't add that extra fraction of an inch room that you need to make your garment fit!

SEWING A SEAM WITH A SERGED EDGE

MACHINE SETTINGS
3- or 4-thread serging

Thread tensions	
Left needle:	3
Right needle:	3
Upper looper:	3
Lower looper:	3
Stitch length:	2–3
Stitch width:	Any
Knife:	Activated
Foot:	Standard foot

1 Place your fabric pieces right sides together and pin at right angles to the edge of the fabric. Sew a seam on your sewing machine $5/8$in (1.5cm) from the edge of the fabric. You will see markings on the needle plate of the machine that will enable you to keep your seam straight.

2 Press the seam to one side using an iron—check the setting matches your chosen fabric.

USING HEAVIER FABRICS OR AVOIDING A BULKY SEAM

If your fabric is heavyweight or bulky, the seam allowances may need to be serged separately instead of together.

1 Place your fabric pieces right sides together and pin at right angles to the edge of the fabric. Sew a seam on your sewing machine ⅝in (1.5cm) from the edge of the fabric. You will see markings on the needle plate of the machine that will enable you to keep your seam straight.

2 Press the seam allowance open. Serge each seam allowance separately, cutting off just the fraying edge of the fabric. This type of seam finish is best for heavier fabrics where a bulky seam would be noticeable.

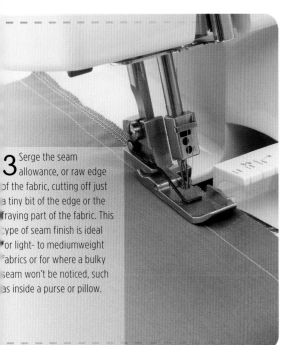

3 Serge the seam allowance, or raw edge of the fabric, cutting off just a tiny bit of the edge or the fraying part of the fabric. This type of seam finish is ideal for light- to mediumweight fabrics or for where a bulky seam won't be noticed, such as inside a purse or pillow.

IDEAS FILE

1. **Deal with very heavy fabrics:** First finish them on the serger and then stitch together on a regular sewing machine.

2. **Make a strong, fine finish:** A narrow serged edge on light- to mediumweight fabrics creates a neat, fine finish and uses less thread than the 4-thread stitch. The sewing machine stitching keeps the seam strong without the need for the additional thread on the serger.

3. **Make seams on a heavy denim skirt:** When using heavy denim or other bulky fabrics, stitch first on the machine and then press the seam open on the inside of the skirt and serge the seam allowances separately. This will reduce bulk in the hem and sides of the garment.

4. **Avoid stitching:** With a lightweight fabric, you can narrow seam finish without stitching first on the sewing machine.

5. **Handle jersey seams:** You can easily stitch seams in jersey with the serger. This technique enables you to match up stripes perfectly without even trying.

Working with heavy fabrics

If you want to create a flat, non-bulky seam on heavy fabrics, it can be tricky to press a seam flat and then serge both seam allowances, as there is not always enough room under the foot to allow the fabrics through. Serge these fabrics first separately and then sew them together on the sewing machine. They can be pressed flat once sewn.

Pressing seams

Seams should always be pressed once they are sewn. Don't wait until you have finished the garment, as it becomes more difficult to press them properly.

Serging around corners

You have now mastered the basic seams and stitches on the serger—but what happens when you get to a corner? On a sewing machine you learn to leave the needle in the fabric and pivot at a corner to stitch around the edge, but this technique won't work on the serger. There are methods you can try and test out to see which will work best for you and your fabric. As always, do a practice test first and see if you like the results.

SERGING OUTSIDE CORNERS

There are times when you might need to serge an outside corner: to finish off a piece of fabric for a table runner, on a throw, or to edge finish a placemat. Try out the different methods outlined here to see which one works best for you.

STOP AND START AGAIN

An easy way to serge outside corners is just to sew along one edge until you reach the end, chain off, cut the thread, and then start again, serging the next side. This method may leave you with a number of chain ends that may need to be finished off, but it is a quick and easy method to use.

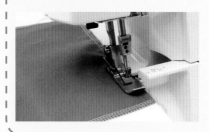

1 Serge one edge of your fabric as usual, chaining off at the end, and then cutting the thread. Don't worry about securing the thread chain—you will be serging over this at the next stage.

2 Position your fabric under the serger to stitch and edge finish the second side. As you begin, cut off the thread chain from step 1. Continue along the edge until it is complete, chain off, and then cut the thread.

3 Now serge along the third and final edges of the rectangle, cutting the thread chain from the previous side as you begin sewing. Choose a suitable secure finish for your ends. In the image at the top of the page, the ends were threaded under the stitches using a bodkin.

CONTINUOUS STITCHING

This method is a bit more difficult but, with some practice, can result in a neater finish, with only one thread chain to secure once you have finished.

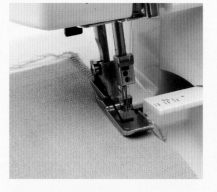

1 Begin sewing the first fabric edge as normal, but stop once you get to the end of the fabric. Don't create a tail end, but stitch just off the fabric by one stitch.

2 Turn the handwheel toward you to lift the needle out of the fabric and raise the presser foot.

CONTINUOUS STITCHING AND SEAM ALLOWANCE

If you are using a seam allowance on your project and need to cut off some of the fabric edge to keep this correct, you should cut a section of the seam allowance off at the start of the second side to make sure that the following stitching is correctly placed. The blade will be unable to cut off the fabric at the start of the row, so you must prepare the edge in advance.

1 Cut a section of seam allowance away from the fabric edge on the second side you will be serging.

2 After you have finished the first side of edging, loosen the needle thread, remove the needle from the fabric by turning the handwheel, and raise the presser foot. Rotate your fabric, line up the stitching to sit on the edge of the fabric, and begin sewing again. The knife blade will continue to cut off the fabric edge, following the same line that you have already cut off.

Tips
• When using the continuous stitching method, don't pull too much slack on the needle thread as this can create a loop in the corners of your project.
• To have a clean finish to your edges, change your sharp corners to curves and go round your fabric in one go, without needing to stop and start again. This will leave you with only one unfinished thread chain, which you can finish using a method of your choice (see Finishing and Securing Ends, page 32).

3 Pull on the needle thread to create some slack and slip the thread off the chain finger.

4 Pivot your work around to the next side and place the needle in the fabric first before lowering the presser foot.

5 Continue serging in this way around all the edges of the project, eventually chaining off and cutting the thread. Secure the remaining thread chain.

SERGING INSIDE CORNERS

There may be occasions when you need to serge inside corners. This is easier to do than keeping a continuous stitch on an outside edge. Essentially the fabric will be stitched in a straight line, folding it away from the inside corner to sit flat and straight with the initial line of stitching.

EDGE FINISHING IN A CONTINUOUS STITCH

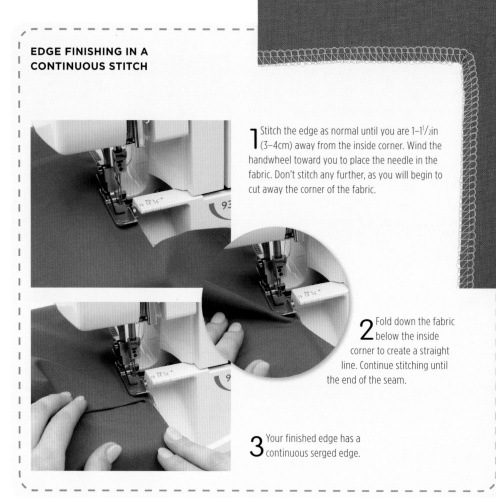

1 Stitch the edge as normal until you are 1–1½in (3–4cm) away from the inside corner. Wind the handwheel toward you to place the needle in the fabric. Don't stitch any further, as you will begin to cut away the corner of the fabric.

2 Fold down the fabric below the inside corner to create a straight line. Continue stitching until the end of the seam.

3 Your finished edge has a continuous serged edge.

SERGING A SEAM IN A CONTINUOUS STITCH

On some occasions you may be cutting off the seam allowance to create a seam and therefore stitching further over into the fabric than when you are just edge finishing. This method also works better for heavier fabrics.

1 Reinforce the inside corner of the seam by stitching just inside the seam line with a regular straight stitch on the sewing machine.

2 Clip into the corner up to the stitching line.

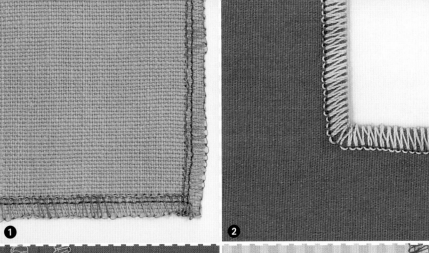

① ②

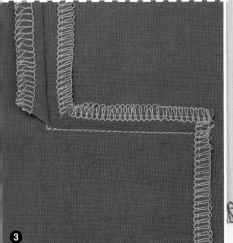

③ ④

IDEAS FILE

1. **Edge finish placemats and tablecloths:** Using the continuous stitch technique (left) will give you a neater finish and leave only one end to secure.

2. **Make a decorative neckline:** Use a continuous stitch to create a flawless finish on your garments.

3. **Edge finish along a vent pleat:** Use a continous stitch to edge finish along a vent pleat. Use this technique for skirts, dresses, and jackets.

4. **Stop and start:** When your seam will be on the inside of a project, like on this pillowcase, use the stop and start method (page 52) to go around the corners. It's the easiest method and nobody will know the difference.

3 Serge up to the corner, hold fabric back to make a straight line, and then continue stitching to the end of the seam or edge.

Front

4 The result is a continuous serged edge. The reinforced line of stitching is barely noticeable under the serging thread.

Tip
For fabrics that don't fray or rip very easily or are made from strong fibers, you can omit the reinforced stitching and just clip the edge.

Reverse

Serging curves, circles, and tubes

When constructing garments, you will often need to serge a curved edge such as a facing on the inside of a garment, a tube for sleeves or legs, a curved neckline, or a hem edge of a skirt. These can be finished more easily on the serger than on the sewing machine alone. The serged stitch will stop the edge from stretching out of shape, and can be turned under and topstitched on a sewing machine to finish a hem or neckline without puckering. The serged stitching also gives a good line to follow when turning up a hem.

> **Tip**
> If the serged edge will be turned under and stitched on the sewing machine to create a hem, just cut the thread ends and pull. There is no need to use any other securing method, as the serging can be sewn over to secure.

GETTING STARTED

Sewing along a curve or around a circle can be a bit tricky, and may require a bit of practice to keep it nice and smooth. It's much easier to sew larger, wider curves than it is to sew smaller ones, since you can almost sew straight on a wide curve. Practice with only a slight curve to gain control over the fabric and your serger before attempting smaller, tighter curves.

Pant legs and sleeves will need edge finishing—either to leave as the finished edge or before hemming on the sewing machine. It can sometimes be difficult to know where on the tube to start or indeed how to finish.

SERGING IN CIRCLES

There are two main techniques to use when your serging will start and end in the same place, which are described at right and over the page. The choice of method will depend on whether you will be cutting off any seam allowance or not. Choosing how to finish the threads at the end will also depend on where the edge will be. If you are edging the bottom of a skirt or a placemat and this will be the finished edge that you will see, then you want to achieve a really neat finish. On most other occasions, such as for sleeves or pant hems, the serging will be turned in and stitched again, so you can leave the finish a little less perfect.

TECHNIQUE 1:
SERGING WITHOUT CUTTING AROUND A TUBE SHAPE

This technique is perfect for creating sleeves and pant legs when you don't want to cut off any excess fabric. This method can be used to give a finish to an exposed edge or can be turned over again and stitched on a sewing machine to neaten the hem.

1 Begin sewing at a joining seam on the fabric edge. You don't need to lift the foot to begin; just push the fabric edge up to the foot on a sideways angle and the feed dog teeth will draw the fabric into the machine.

SERGING AN INSIDE CURVE

To sew an inside curve, you must begin sewing from one edge. Don't lift up the foot—just push the fabric up to the feed dog teeth and the machine will guide it under the needle. As you sew, guide the fabric toward the cutting blade, positioning the fabric so that you sew straight. Don't force the fabric under the foot or it may end up puckered. The finished serging should sit flat and not produce a wavy edge. Check your machine settings if you find that the edge is gathered or ruffled.

As you sew inside curves, keep your eye on the seam allowance and try to feed the fabric slowly and evenly into the machine. If the cutting blade is engaged, aim to cut off an even amount all the way around the curve. If you are sewing a rolled hem or have disengaged the knife, try to keep the edge of the fabric aligned in the same place or you could end up with a wobbly edge.

SERGING AN OUTSIDE CURVE

Outside curves need more practice than inside curves to keep your stitching on the edge. Sew slowly, keeping control of the fabric as it feeds into the machine. If you feel your fabric is going out of place, lift up the foot, reposition, and continue sewing.

2 Continue sewing around the tube, keeping the edging even and without cutting off any fabric other than fraying threads.

3 Once you reach the starting point, continue to serge over the beginning of the thread for a few stitches. Then pull the fabric out of the machine to one side, stitching a chain end before cutting the thread and securing the ends.

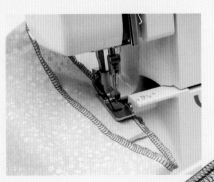

4 For the neatest finish, only oversew the beginning threads by one or two stitches. Lift up the foot and raise the needles. Pull the fabric from under the foot and chain off without stitching again on your fabric. Cut the threads. Thread the ends onto a needle and bury under the stitching. Bury the thread into the wrong side of the fabric.

TECHNIQUE 2:
SERGING AND CUTTING OFF SEAM ALLOWANCE

To cut off an even amount of seam allowance around a tube, curve, or circle, there are two methods that can be used. This first method will give a neater finish, as the stitching won't overlap much when you come to the end. Use this method for exposed edges, such as decorative hems on skirts or sleeves.

1 Cut out a small section (1in/2–3cm) of the seam allowance from the straightest edge.

3 When you return to the beginning, serge only over a few stitches before chaining off and cutting the threads. Secure the threads by tying them in a knot and using a needle to bury the thread ends into the serging—not too much, as this can make the edge finishing appear messy.

2 Lift the foot up and place your fabric under it, beginning at the gap in the fabric. Lower the foot and begin sewing around the edge of the fabric, cutting off the seam allowance.

TECHNIQUE 2:
ALTERNATIVE METHOD

For a quicker but slightly messier finish, use this method—great for when you want to quickly serge an edge that will be turned over and stitched again. If the serged stitching won't be seen, there's no need for a perfect finish.

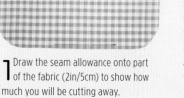

1 Draw the seam allowance onto part of the fabric (2in/5cm) to show how much you will be cutting away.

2 Begin serging with the foot down, angling in from the right. Gradually cut away the seam allowance until the blade lines up with the line drawn onto the fabric. Continue sewing, keeping the fabric edge in line with a stitching line guide, or using your eyes to judge and keep the seam line even all the way around.

3 Continue serging until you reach the beginning again, looking for the line on the fabric to make sure you cut off the same seam allowance all the way around. Serge over the first two or three stitches and then pull the fabric out from under the foot. Chain off and then cut the threads. Secure the thread ends.

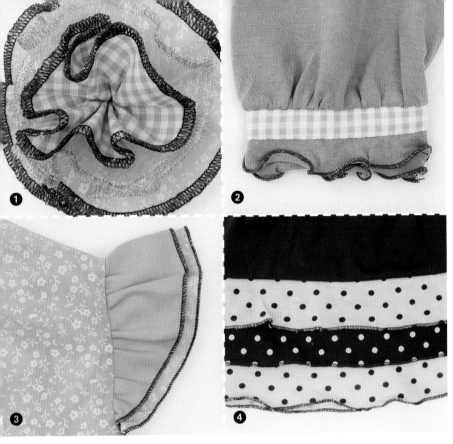

①

②

③

④

IDEAS FILE

1. **Create decorative circles:** Serge many circles of fabric and then stitch these together in the center. Use a rolled hemming technique set to a short stitch and create a lettuce-leaf edge to give more volume to the circles. They could be used for decorative flowers, wrist corsages for bridesmaids, or fascinators. Insert fine wire into the edge to add more shape.

2. **Finish your cuffs:** Use a contrasting thread and narrow hem setting to finish your cuffs. Adjust the differential feed and stitch length for better coverage and more volume.

3. **Decorate sleeves:** Add a contrast hem edge to your sleeves by using a rolled or narrow hem finish.

4. **Add a decorative hem:** Use a narrow hem setting on your machine to create a lettuce-leaf edging for the hem of a skirt.

SERGING QUICK CIRCLES

To create serged circles of fabric, use a narrow hem setting and 2-thread or 3-thread serge stitch to finish the edges of your fabric. For heavier fabrics, choose a wider stitch. There's no need to cut the circles out of the fabric first—just cut a cardstock template and let your serger cut the fabric.

1 Cut circles out of cardstock or heavy paper. Use a pair of compasses or draw around a plate, pot, or bowl to get your perfect circle shape. Pin or stick the circles to your fabric using masking tape wrapped over itself.

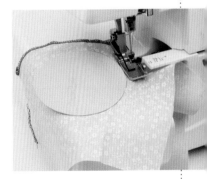

3 Stitch on the serger, with the cardstock circle next to the left side of the foot. The blade will cut off any excess fabric.

4 When you get to the starting stitches, serge over two to three stitches and then pull the fabric out to the left. Chain off and cut the threads. Secure the ends by threading the chain end into the serging stitches on the wrong side of the fabric.

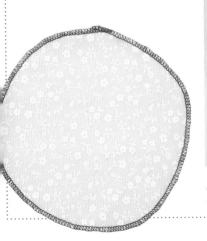

2 Push the fabric up to the foot and begin stitching.

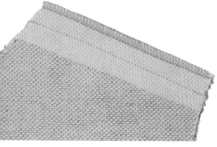

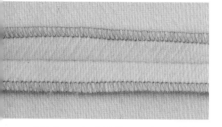

Strips of interfacing on the shoulder seam of a jacket.

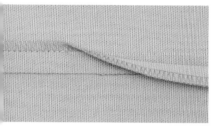

On bulky, woolen fabric the seam is serged before stitching on a sewing machine.

A welt seam is used to give additional strength to a purse seam.

Stabilizing seams

The seams or edge finishes of some projects will need extra strength and stability. This is important for seams that will come under stress, such as the crotch of pants, shoulder seams, or underarm seams of coats. Purses, depending on their function, may also need extra-strong seams so that they can withstand heavy items being carried in them. Garment edges will need more stability at the neck or waistline.

INTERFACING
Interfacing is often used to stabilize and add structure to cuffs, collars, and waistbands. It comes in different weights and as sew-in or iron-in options. Choosing the right interfacing for your project will depend on the fabric you are using. Select interfacing that is a similar weight to your fabric. Strips of interfacing can be ironed onto a seam before serging to add strength.

MACHINE STITCHING
Sewing the seam on the sewing machine, either before or after you have serged, is another way of adding extra strength. Welt, fell, and French seams (see pages 64–67) can add more strength to a project, allowing it to be worn and washed repeatedly without falling apart.

TWILL TAPE
Serging over twill tape, yarn, or ribbon will make the seam or fabric edge much more stable and strong. Depending on which technique you use, it can also add decoration.

A French seam will add strength and a neat finish to a silk blouse.

Tip
Serging over ribbon can add decoration to your seams. Twill tape usually only comes in black or white, so using a brightly colored ribbon can add a flash of color, as well as strength, to your seams.

USING TWILL TAPE

MACHINE SETTINGS
3- or 4-thread serging (using either needle)

Thread tensions
Left needle: 3
Right needle: 3
Lower looper: 3
Upper knife: 3

Stitch length: 2–3 depending on fabric choice
Stitch width: Adjust for stitch type
Knife: Activated
Foot: Standard or taping attachment

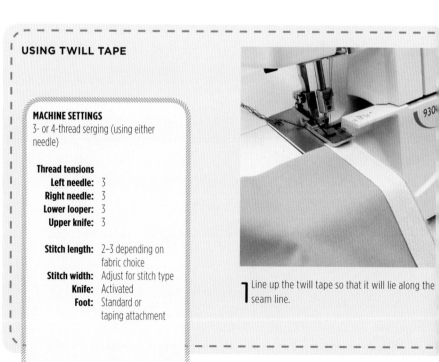

1 Line up the twill tape so that it will lie along the seam line.

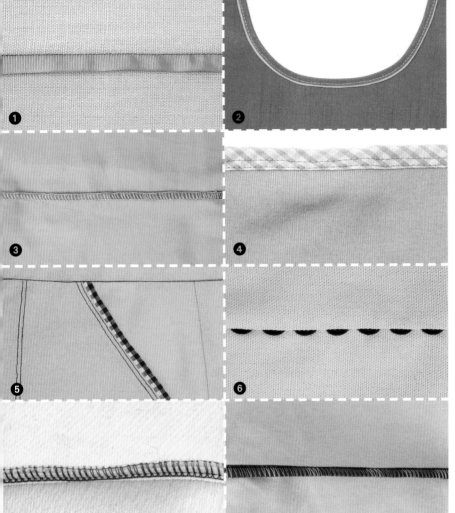

IDEAS FILE

1. **Use ribbon to decorate a purse:** Use grosgrain ribbon on the outside of a purse to add strength to the seams and decoration to the project.

2. **Use bias binding around a neckline:** Bias-cut binding works brilliantly on curves and adds decoration. Here, an extra bias-cut strip has been inserted between the layers for interest.

3. **Use yarn as a stabilizer:** Multicolored, chunky yarn is serged into the seam to add strength and decoration.

4. **Attach binding using the cover stitch:** Bias binding is attached using a cover stitch to keep a neckline edge from stretching.

5. **Use binding at a pocket edge:** Add strength to pockets while forming a decorative trim.

6. **Decorate a purse:** Use wide rickrack to stabilize a purse seam and give a decorative edge.

7. **Try using tricot tape:** When working with jersey or stretch fabrics, try using tricot tape to stabilize your seams. It is ideal for underwear, nightwear, or T-shirts.

8. **Serge over ribbon:** For added strength and interest, serge over ribbon to create decorative seams on the inside or outside of a project.

3 The finished seam will ensure strength and hold in place securely.

2 Serge as normal. The stitches will hold the twill tape in place, stitching over a narrow tape or through a wide one. Trim off any fraying edges only.

Mock band hems

This is a really quick and easy way to finish a hem. It appears as if a separate band of matching fabric has been stitched to the edge of your project or garment, but it is actually created in a much simpler way. Use this technique to finish garments with ease, giving the appearance of an added cuff on a sleeve, or band of fabric at the bottom of a top, skirt, or dress.

WHY CHOOSE A MOCK BAND HEM

The mock band hem can be used as a simpler alternative to the blind hem (see pages 84–85). A blind hem is one that is barely visible from the right side of the fabric but it can be difficult to achieve. The mock band hem won't be "blind" but it can save you time in trying to create an invisible hem by making a statement of it.

It works really well on jersey fabrics, where hemming can sometimes be a bit tricky. The mock band hem does not require as much precision with sewing the hem, so it is great if you want to finish something quickly or if you're a beginner to serging. This technique can be done with a standard foot, so there is no need for additional attachments.

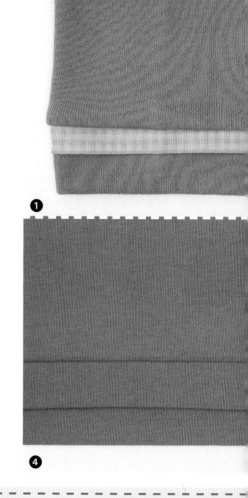

❶

❹

CREATING THE MOCK BAND HEM

MACHINE SETTINGS

4- or 3-thread serging (using either needle)

Thread tensions	
Left needle:	3
Right needle:	3
Upper looper:	3
Lower looper:	3
Stitch length:	2–3
Stitch width:	Adjust to suit your hem—wider for heavier fabrics and narrower for light- or mediumweight fabrics
Knife:	Activated
Foot:	Standard

1 Turn up the edge of the fabric to the wrong side. Make sure that the edge is even all the way along the hem. Pin the hem in place.

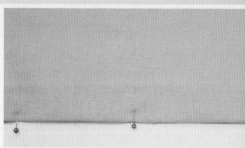

2 Press the hem, taking the pins out as you iron so as not to mark or indent the fabric.

3 Turn the folded hem edge back toward the right side of the fabric, so that the raw edge of the fabric is level with the new fold. Pin in place.

② ③

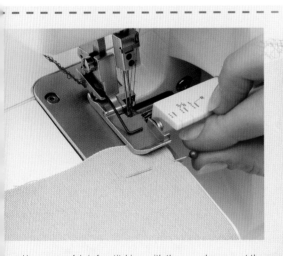

⑤ ⑥

IDEAS FILE

1. **Decorate a cuff with ribbon:** Enclose some ribbon between right sides of the fabric in the folded edge when following step 3, below. When you serge the hem and fold back, the ribbon will add a pretty feature to your hem or cuffs.

2. **Add a ruffle:** Serge the edge and gather a piece of fabric before inserting this into the folded edge when following step 3, below.

3. **Reverse the technique:** Fold the fabric in the opposite direction, making the wrong side of the technique appear on the right side for added decoration.

4. **Use folds:** Add a number of folds to your fabric above the hem for extra interest.

5. **Add style to a pocket:** The reverse side of the technique is used here to show off the decorative thread.

6. **Finish a jersey skirt:** For a quick and easy finish, use the mock band hem for a jersey skirt.

5 Sew evenly along the edge keeping the serging straight. Once you finish the seam, chain off, cut the thread, and secure the ends. Open up the fold and lay the fabric flat. Press the hemming stitches up away from the fold of the hem.

4 Line up your fabric for stitching, with the raw edge nearest the cutting blade. Position the fabric so that the needle will sew into the fold, only cutting off any fraying threads. Don't forget to remove the pins as you sew.

Reverse

Front

French seams

A French seam is a type of self-enclosed seam where the seam allowances are bound within the final stitching. Because the seam is sewn twice it gives added strength to the stitching, making it hardwearing.

Tips
• Test the technique first. If you are trying to keep your seam allowances correct, you will need to make sure that you don't stitch the first part on too wide a stitch setting.
• For sheer fabrics, use a thread that is the same color (or as close as possible) to your fabric. This way, you won't be able to see the serging stitches through the fabric.

Using the chain stitch setting

If your machine has a chain stitch setting, you can use the serger instead of the sewing machine to add the stitch lines. See page 72 for more on the chain stitch.

WHEN TO USE A FRENCH SEAM

A French seam is sewn first from the right side and then again from the wrong side. The first line of stitching is sewn on the serger and the second using the sewing machine. It is perfect for sheer fabrics where you don't want to see the stitching through the fabric, or for visible seams on unlined garments such as jackets. It is also ideal for childrenswear, as the thread on the seam allowance won't rub against the skin. The technique also adds strength to keep seams secure when garments will be washed and worn many times. Using this technique when making purses will keep the inside neat and avoid the need for lining. You can even make your purses reversible, as the French seam will look good from the insides, too.

SERGING A FRENCH SEAM

1 Place the fabric pieces wrong sides together and serge the edge, using a 3-thread stitch. A 4-thread stitch will create a wider seam once finished and can be used for heavier fabrics to add more strength. For a really narrow finish on sheer fabrics, use a 2-thread serging stitch.

2 Press the seam flat to embed the stitches and then press again to one side.

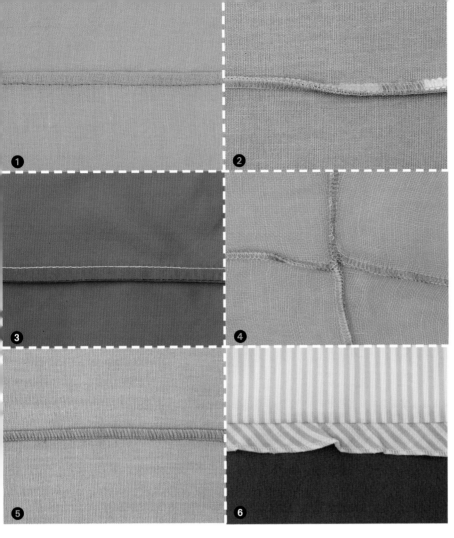

1. **Create a delicate finish:** Use 2-thread serging before stitching again on the sewing machine. This technique is used here on a kaftan seam.

2. **Create a raised French seam:** Sew the seam first using a 2- or 3-thread stitch on the serger, and then again using a 4-thread stitch. Here, a heavy yarn was used in the upper looper for added color on one side of the seam, and stitching over a ribbon on the other side of the seam.

3. **Finish a lightweight lining:** Use 3-thread serging and a sewing machine for a neat finish.

4. **Make your purse seam decorative:** Begin by sewing right sides together, then finishing the enclosed seam on the outside for decoration.

5. **Create a simple raised seam:** For added strength, serge the seam twice: first from the outside, then again from the inside. This is great for purses or seams that need extra durability.

6. **Insert a ruffle:** Add your ruffle in step 1, below, placing the ruffle with its wrong side to the right side of the fabric. The raw edge will be enclosed at step 4, below, keeping it secured in the seam.

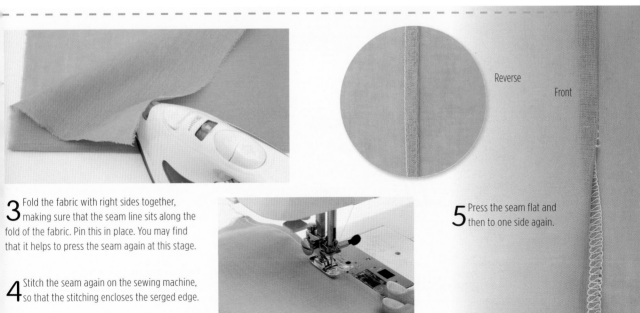

3 Fold the fabric with right sides together, making sure that the seam line sits along the fold of the fabric. Pin this in place. You may find that it helps to press the seam again at this stage.

4 Stitch the seam again on the sewing machine, so that the stitching encloses the serged edge.

5 Press the seam flat and then to one side again.

Reverse

Front

Welt and fell seams

Welt and fell seams are great for adding additional strength to a garment or purse. You usually see this type of seam on jeans, sportswear, or other items that need to be more hardwearing.

CHOOSING A WELT OR FELL SEAM

To create these types of seam, you need to use both your sewing machine and your serger—unless you have a machine that is able to stitch a chain or cover stitch, and then these settings can be used instead. These two types of seam are often confused because, once finished, they can look almost identical. The welt seam is sewn first with right sides together and the fell seam is sewn first with wrong sides together. The reverse side of the fell seam will usually appear neater than that of the welt seam.

Welt seams are created on the inside of the garment or wrong side of a project. You can sew the seam first on the sewing machine for bulky fabrics, or go straight ahead and serge with right sides together, then press and topstitch the seam flat.

A fell seam is formed on the outside or right side of your project. It gives the appearance of flatlocking (see pages 74–75) and is best used in place of flatlocking for heavier fabrics that won't lie flat or that fray easily. Alternatively, stitch first on the sewing machine, trim one side of the seam allowance as shown for the welt seam, then fold the wider seam allowance over. Fold at the raw edge and enclose the trimmed edge.

Tip

Try using a fusible thread in the lower looper. You may not need to topstitch the seam in place once it is pressed to one side. Place wax paper over the serging when pressing to avoid fusible threads sticking to the iron.

CREATING A FELL SEAM

1 Place wrong sides of fabric together and serge the seam using 3 or 4 threads, depending on the strength needed in the seam.

2 Press the serging to one side and use the sewing machine to topstitch the seam in place, sewing close to the fabric edge.

CREATING A WELT SEAM

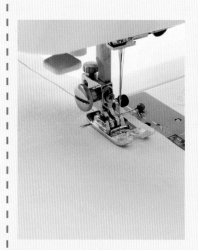

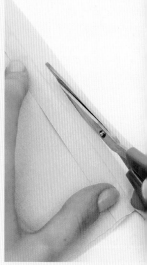

1 Place right sides of fabric together and sew a $5/8$in (1.5cm) seam on the sewing machine.

2 Trim one seam allowance to $1/4$in (6mm).

IDEAS FILE

1. **Create a clean finish on your fell seam:** Turn in the serged edge so that the seam allowance is enclosed, then stitch flat on the sewing machine.
2. **Try contrasting threads:** Add detail on a fell seam with a serged and machine-sewn edge.
3. **Triple topstitch:** Use a cover stitch machine to add in 3 rows of different-colored stitching to keep seams secure and decorative.
4. **Add detail:** Use a welt seam on the panels of a shirt to add detail.
5. **Insert lace:** Add decoration with lace placed under the folded edge of a fell seam and then topstitched in place.
6. **Create a chain-stitch finish:** Combine a welt seam with chain stitch for skirt seams.

Tip

If your serger has a chain-stitch setting, use this to add the topstitching or, alternatively, use the cover-hem setting to add two rows of stitching in one go.

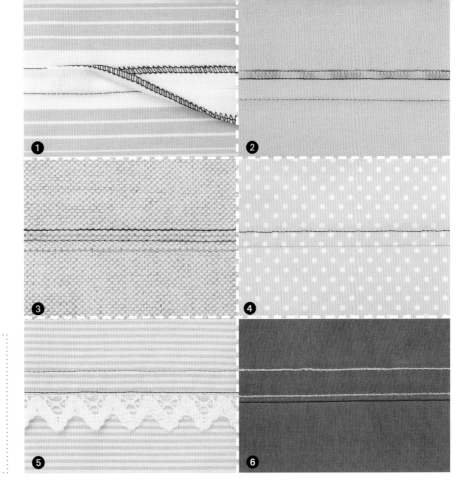

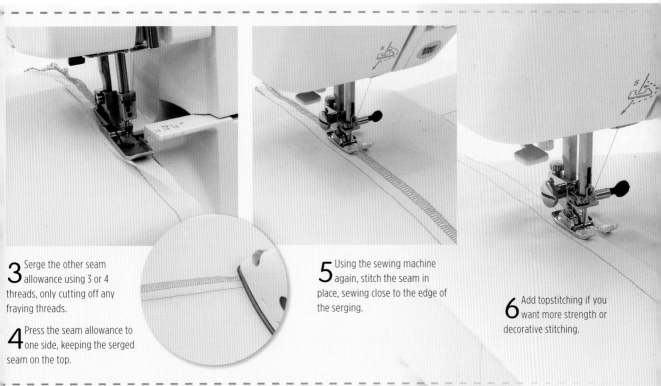

3 Serge the other seam allowance using 3 or 4 threads, only cutting off any fraying threads.

4 Press the seam allowance to one side, keeping the serged seam on the top.

5 Using the sewing machine again, stitch the seam in place, sewing close to the edge of the serging.

6 Add topstitching if you want more strength or decorative stitching.

Roll hemming

Sometimes you will need a narrow stitch to create a hem or add detail to a garment. A rolled hem works best on light- to mediumweight fabrics to create a delicate yet strong edge finish. Most serging machines have a special setting to create a rolled hem and can be adjusted relatively easily for this type of stitching. The stitch is formed from the right needle and one or two loopers. The most common rolled hem is formed with 3 threads. Remove the left needle to ensure that the stitch forms correctly and that the needle does not leave unwanted holes in the fabric.

Check your manual for instructions on removing the stitch finger on your machine. On this Janome 9300X, the knife blade must be disengaged before you slide the pink needle plate setting knob from S (standard serging/above) to R (rolled hemming/below).

ADJUSTING YOUR MACHINE

Most machines will have a removable stitch finger, which can be moved out of the way with a lever so that you can change the settings to a narrow stitch width. Set the right needle slightly tighter than normal and tighten the lower looper thread. The lower looper thread will pull the upper looper thread to the back of the fabric, rolling the fabric edge at the same time. When the lower looper is adjusted to a looser setting, the result is a narrow hem finish without a rolled edge.

The knife is then moved back into the activated position before serging. Other machines may have different mechanisms that will move the stitch finger without the knife being moved first.

2- or 3-thread serging?

If you can't get the right finish on your chosen fabric using the 3-thread rolled hem setting, change to the 2-thread setting and see if the results are any better.

STITCHING A ROLL HEM

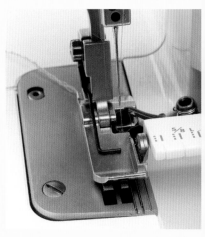

MACHINE SETTINGS
2- or 3-thread serging (using the right needle)

Thread tensions	
Right needle:	4
Upper looper:	3
Lower looper:	7
Stitch length:	R
Stitch width:	Narrow
Knife:	Activated
Foot:	Standard foot

1 Refer to your manual and set the machine up for roll hemming by adjusting the tension dials and removing the stitch finger as necessary.

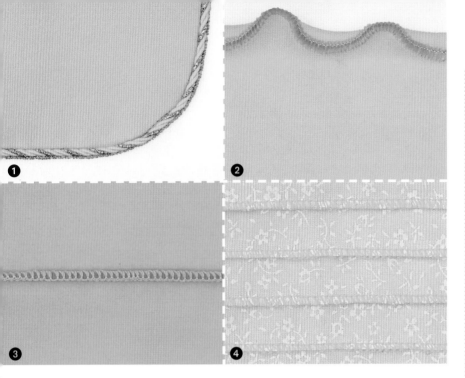

① ② ③ ④

Tips
• The serger used for this technique has an "R" setting for stitch length. Depending on the finish required, this could be set from a short satin stitch setting to slightly longer. For a picot edging use a longer stitch length (3–4), so that the pulling and rolling of the edge forms little decorative bumps on the edges of the fabric.
• Test the stitch on scrap fabric first. Adjust the tension settings until the lower looper thread appears as a straight stitch on the reverse of the fabric, barely seen from the right side.

IDEAS FILE
1. **Finish placemats:** Create a rolled hem over cord to create raised detail.
2. **Create a lettuce-leaf edging:** Lower the stitch length and differential feed or stretch the fabric as you stitch to give a decorative edge to skirt hems and ruffles. Using woolly nylon will give the best coverage.

3. **Finish seams on sheer fabrics:** A rolled hem will create a tiny, neat finish.
4. **Create pin tucks on a lightweight blouse:** The seams can be sewn on the right or wrong side of the garment, depending on the finish required.

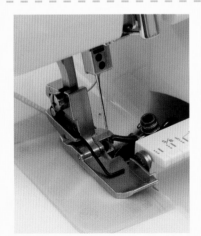

2 Begin stitching as normal, pushing the fabric up to the foot and lowering your foot onto the pedal.

3 Once finished, chain off, cut the threads, and secure the ends. The finished stitch should be an even, tight roll on the edge of the fabric.

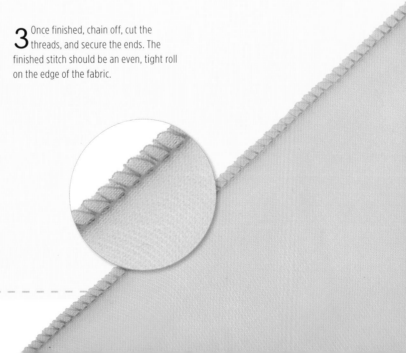

Cover stitch

The cover stitch makes a double or triple row of parallel straight stitching on the top side of the fabric with a serged finish on the underside. It is most commonly used on knitted fabrics for hemming and adds topstitching while finishing the raw edge on a hem at the same time. The stitch can also stretch, making it a much better finish than just straight stitching on a regular sewing machine.

COVER STITCH SERGERS

A basic serger will not have this function; it is only found on specific cover-stitch machines or on mid- to top-range multifunction machines. The setting for the stitch is usually a wide or narrow cover stitch. Some machines also offer a triple hem function or a top cover stitch, which shows loops on the top and underside of the fabric as it is sewn. This stitch is not restricted to hemming, but can be used to add rows of decorative stitches on garments, purses, or pillows.

Check your machine manual to see how to set up this stitch. Test it on a scrap piece of fabric to ensure that the tension is correctly balanced and that you achieve the width of stitch

desired for your project. Sew heavier fabrics with a longer stitch and light- or mediumweight fabrics with a stitch length of 2.5 or above.

On some store-bought garments, the cover stitch is used to form the hem and the side seams of the garment are stitched last. For a neater finish on a homemade garment, sew the hem last. This will ensure that the finished edge of the side seam is partly enclosed within the cover stitch.

JOINING A CIRCLE OR TUBE WITH THE COVER STITCH

If you are sewing in a tube, continue stitching over the beginning stitches as you complete your tube. Use the thread tension lever or pull on the needle threads to release some tension. Pull the fabric out to the back of the machine, cut the threads, and secure these by tying a knot or threading through the stitches. On a cover-stitch machine, remove the extension table if you can to allow you to sew narrow tubes more easily.

Tip
Use an adjustable seam guide or hemming guide to help keep stitching straight.

HEMMING WITH THE COVER STITCH

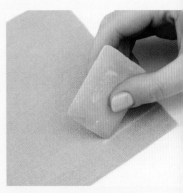

1 Turn under the hem to the desired width and pin in place. Press the hem in place, removing the pins as you go to avoid marking or indenting the fabric.

2 Place the fabric right side up and mark with chalk or disappearing marker pen where the edge of the fabric is on the underside.

①   **②**   **③**   **④**

⑤   **⑥**   **⑦**   **⑧**

IDEAS FILE

1. **Hem a knit fabric:** Use the cover stitch to give a professional finish to the hem of a knit fabric skirt.

2. **Decorate a pillowcase:** Use the triple cover stitch and different colored threads for the edging of a pillowcase.

3. **Attach lace pieces together:** Use cover stitch and water-soluble stabilizer.

4. **Insert a zipper:** Use cover stitch to insert a zipper quickly and securely. Use a longer zipper than required, position with the zip pull extending 1–2 inches (2.5–5cm) above the opening, and stitch in place.

5. **Add texture to a pillow:** Thread cord through the loops on the reverse side of the cover stitch, or stitch over cord running along the underside of the fabric to create a raised, trapunto effect.

6. **Finish a neckline:** Use a stabilizer on the reverse to stop stretching, and cover stitch on the right side for a neat finish.

7. **Decorate:** Use cover stitch on the wrong side of the fabric or top cover stitch on the right side, to create rows of decorative stitching. Metallic or bold threads will add interest.

8. **Create pin tucks:** Add detail to a pocket by using the cover stitch for a pin-tuck effect. Stitch the pocket in place using cover stitch, too.

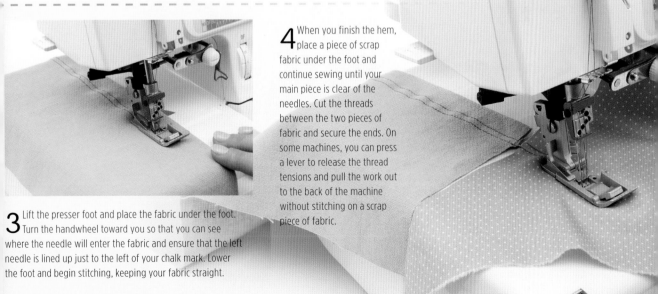

3 Lift the presser foot and place the fabric under the foot. Turn the handwheel toward you so that you can see where the needle will enter the fabric and ensure that the left needle is lined up just to the left of your chalk mark. Lower the foot and begin stitching, keeping your fabric straight.

4 When you finish the hem, place a piece of scrap fabric under the foot and continue sewing until your main piece is clear of the needles. Cut the threads between the two pieces of fabric and secure the ends. On some machines, you can press a lever to release the thread tensions and pull the work out to the back of the machine without stitching on a scrap piece of fabric.

Chain stitch

Chain stitch is formed with one looper and one needle. On the right side, the stitch appears like a straight stitch; on the reverse of the fabric, a chain is formed. The needle thread should only just be seen on the reverse side.

CREATING CHAIN STITCH ON YOUR SERGER

This function is not available on all machines, as it requires a special looper to create the stitch, but it is usually found on most mid-range multifunction machines and also on cover-stitch machines. On multifunction machines it can be fussy to adjust the machine settings to create a chain stitch but, just as when you first started using the serger, everything gets quicker and easier the more you do it.

On cover-stitch machines, it is easy to change to the chain-stitch function—you just have to remove the threads from all but one needle and then remove the needles that you are not using.

Check your machine manual to find out how to change your machine settings to create a chain stitch. You will probably need to unthread the loopers and then thread up a lower looper specifically designed for chain stitch. The needles may also need adjusting to a new position and then rethreading. On some machines, part of the looper cover will need replacing to form a sewing table.

TURNING CORNERS WITH CHAIN STITCH

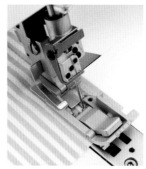

1 Make the last stitch to the turning point by using the handwheel. Turn the handwheel again so the needle eye is above the fabric but the needle tip is still in the fabric. Lift the foot and pivot the fabric.

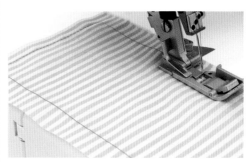

2 Lower the foot again and continue stitching.

USING CHAIN STITCH

If your machine is not happy producing chain stitch without fabric, begin by stitching on scrap fabric until an even stitch is produced. Then change to sewing on your project. At the end, stitch on scrap fabric again and then cut the threads between fabric pieces.

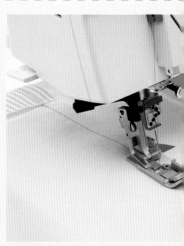

MACHINE SETTINGS
2-thread chain stitch (using one of far left needle settings on multifunctional machine)

Thread tensions
Left needle:	Neutral
Chain looper:	Neutral
Stitch length:	3 (or longer as desired)
Stitch width:	N/A
Knife:	Disengaged
Foot:	Standard foot or clear chain-stitch foot

1 Lift the foot, place the scrap fabric underneath, and then lower the foot into position. Stitch on scrap fabric, adjusting the dials to correct the tension as necessary.

2 Begin sewing on your project, butting the project fabric up to the scrap fabric.

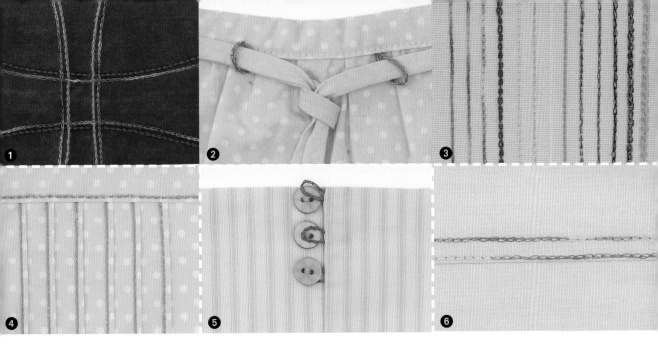

IDEAS FILE

1. **Decorate a pillow cover:** Decorative thread used in the looper creates an interesting chain stitch on the underside of the fabric.

2. **Create belt loops:** Chain stitch without fabric to create loops and use these for belt loops. To make these belt loops more secure, create three or more chains and braid these together.

3. **Use upside-down chain:** Using decorative thread in the needle produces an uneven slub-like decorative chain underneath. Stitch on the wrong side of the fabric, so that this can be seen on the right side of your project. Loosen the needle thread to allow this to show more prominently on the reverse side.

4. **Make decorative pin tucks:** Use chain stitch with contrasting threads.

5. **Make button loops:** Use chain stitch without fabric to create a cord for button loops. This technique will also work well as a chain thread for attaching skirt or coat linings to garments.

6. **Add a decorative finish:** Topstitch your seams with chain stitch to add a decorative finish to a garment.

Tip
To create thread chains, try stitching onto dissolvable fabric. Wash away the fabric and you will be left with a chain of threads.

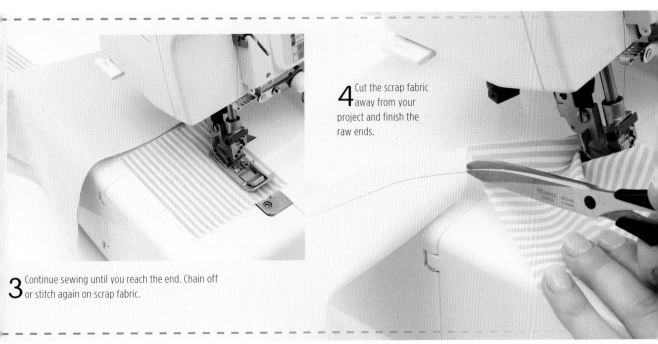

4 Cut the scrap fabric away from your project and finish the raw ends.

3 Continue sewing until you reach the end. Chain off or stitch again on scrap fabric.

Flatlocking

To create a flatlocked stitch, serge two edges, or a fold of fabric, and then pull open so that the stitches lie flat. Flatlocking can be substituted for a regular serged seam to add detail to seam lines on the right side of garments or purses. It works best on heavy or bulky fabrics that don't fray easily.

CHOOSING A STITCH

The flatlock stitch is reversible and can be used on the right or wrong side of a project showing either loops or ladders. Choose different threads to create a range of finishes, making the stitches stand out or blend with the fabric. Flatlocking can be done with 2, 3, or 4 threads. The type of stitch you choose will depend on your machine, the finish you want to achieve, and the type of fabric being used. Many basic sergers can't be set up for 2-thread flatlocking, so use a 3-thread flatlocking stitch instead. Some adjustments will need to be made on the tension of your machine—the needle stitches need to be loose, so that the stitch can be pulled open.

FLATLOCKING HEMS

To create a flatlocked hem, use three threads and follow the instructions for creating a mock band hem (see pages 62–63), but don't cut the folded edge of the fabric with the cutting knife. Disengage the knife to avoid making this mistake or sew slowly and carefully, using the blade to cut only fraying threads.

2- and 4-thread flatlocking

If your machine can perform the 2-thread flatlocking stitch, you will most likely need to use a 2-thread converter to block the eye of the upper looper. This may be built into your machine or be a separate part in your accessory box.

To create 4-thread flatlocking, lower the tension on both needles to 0. The stitch does create a slight bump and can be used to add a feature.

3-THREAD FLATLOCKING FOR SEAMS

Before you start, the needle thread should be as loose as possible and the lower looper thread as tight as possible. The needle thread should be pulled by the looper thread to the edge of the fabric. The top side of the fabric will look like a normal serged edge formed from the looper threads. From the underside, the needle thread should appear as a row of Vs. The upper looper thread may need to be loosened slightly to produce the correct stitch.

1 Place right sides of fabric together, pin, and then stitch in place, cutting off any excess seam allowance as necessary. Don't lift up the foot; just push the fabric up to the foot and the feed dog teeth will pull the fabric into the machine.

MACHINE SETTINGS
3-thread serging (using left needle)

Thread tensions
Left needle: 0
Upper looper: 3 (or looser)
Lower looper: 9

Stitch length: 2–3
Stitch width: Wide or as required
Knife: Activated
Foot: Standard

Tip

To see the ladders on the wrong side, place the wrong sides of fabric together and then flatlock the pieces together as in step 1, above.

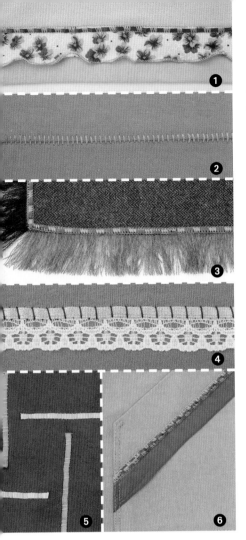

IDEAS FILE

1. **Insert a ruffle:** Roll hem the edge of a narrow piece of fabric to use as a ruffle. Fold the fabric with wrong sides together and line up the ruffle with the raw edge along the fold. Serge and decorate with woven ribbon.

2. **Add interest to cardigan cuffs:** Use a contrasting thread color to add interest to cuffs on a jersey cardigan by creating a flatlocked hem.

3. **Make a fringe:** Create a flatlocked fringe along the edge of a blanket or shawl.

4. **Insert lace:** Add detail to a garment by adding lace to a flatlocked seam.

5. **Make decorative stitching lines:** Fold and stitch multiple times over the fabric of a throw or pillow cover. Add more detail by weaving ribbons through the stitching.

6. **Decorate a pocket:** Add a flatlocked seam and attach ribbon to decorate a pocket on a shirt. Two stripes of narrow ribbon have been woven through the flatlocked threads.

FLATLOCK FRINGE
This technique works best on loosely woven fabrics where the edge can be easily raveled. Set the machine for 3-thread flatlocking and disengage the cutting blade.

1 Fold the fabric edge to the wrong side, turning the edge under for as long as you want the fringe to be. Flatlock over the folded edge.

2 Pull the stitches flat and press flat. Ravel the raw edge of the fabric to create a fringe.

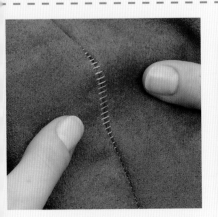

2 Once the seam is finished, chain off, cut the thread, and secure the ends. Open out the finished seam and pull so that the ladders are seen on the right side.

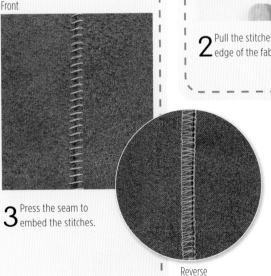

Front

3 Press the seam to embed the stitches.

Reverse

Serging with decorative threads

Show off your serged edges! Using decorative threads can add contrasting edging to your projects. Don't just use matching threads—experiment with different colors and types of thread to add something different to garments and household items.

CHOOSING YOUR THREAD

Try threads you may never have thought of using, such as topstitching thread, metallic thread, skinny ribbon, or even crochet thread. Some of these threads are thicker than usual sewing threads, but it doesn't mean they can't be used. Although many heavier threads won't go through the eye of the needle, they can be used in the loopers quite successfully since the eyes are larger and there are fewer thread guides to cause a strain on the threads or to cause any snapping. The heaviest threads should be used in the upper looper only to avoid any problems.

VARYING THE STITCH LENGTH AND WIDTH

For the best results, start with the widest and longest stitch length and adjust smaller until you get the desired stitch; thicker threads take up more room, so longer and wider stitches need to be used. To create the widest stitch, loosen the tension to the lowest setting on the loopers. It may take some adjusting and experimenting to maintain the best tension for stitching with decorative threads. It is best to adjust one tension dial at a time and see the effects of this before adjusting another. You can use a standard foot for this type of sewing, with no need to buy additional attachments.

Tips
• Before starting to sew, pull threads to the back of the serger and hold these loosely.
• Make sure you sew slowly when starting.
• Always check the size of needle you are using: change to a thicker or thinner needle depending on the thickness of the threads and fabrics that you are using.

SERGING WITH CROCHET THREAD

Crochet thread can be used to add a decorative edge to a project, forming a braid-like fabric edging. Choose your type of thread carefully—it must be soft, pliable, and narrow enough to go through the machine and upper looper.

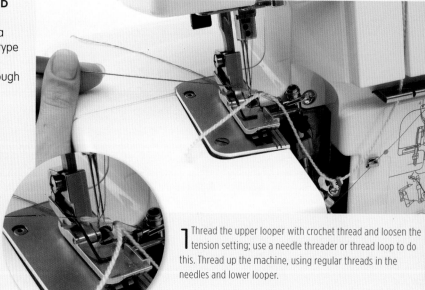

MACHINE SETTINGS
3- or 4-thread serging (using the left needle)

Thread tensions	
Left needle:	3
Right needle:	3
Upper looper:	0
Lower looper:	3
Stitch length:	4 (or as long as possible)
Stitch width:	Widest setting
Knife:	Activated
Foot:	Standard foot

1 Thread the upper looper with crochet thread and loosen the tension setting; use a needle threader or thread loop to do this. Thread up the machine, using regular threads in the needles and lower looper.

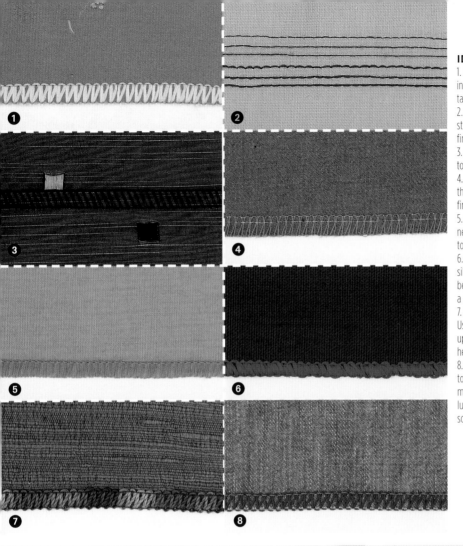

1

2

3

4

5

6

7

8

IDEAS FILE

1. **Add a luxurious silk edging:** Use silk floss in the loopers. This is a beautiful finish for a table runner.

2. **Add interest to plain fabrics:** Use cover stitch in contrasting colors. This is a great finish for a pillowcase.

3. **Add detail to upholstery:** Use flatlocking to create decorative lines.

4. **Add a shimmer to your skirt:** Use metallic thread only in the needles to create a subtle finish for a garment hem.

5. **Create a soft edge:** Use woolly nylon in the needles and loopers to give excellent coverage to the fabric edge.

6. **Decorate an edge:** Use 1/16-in (2-mm) wide silk ribbon in the upper looper to create this beautiful soft finish to your edges—perfect for a tablecloth.

7. **Create a braidlike finish for a throw:** Use heavy, pearlized tapestry cotton in the upper looper only to make a heavier trim for heavier fabrics.

8. **Make your edging stand out:** Use topstitching thread in a striking color or a mediumweight strong thread with a high luster. Thread the upper looper only for something a bit different.

2 Set the machine to the longest stitch settings and turn the flywheel to ensure that stitches are being made. Test out on your fabric and adjust stitch length/tension setting until you achieve the desired result.

3 Sew slowly until you have completed your edge.

Set stitch length to the maximum setting—in this case, 4.

Set the differential feed dial to 1.

FAGOTING

A type of fagoting stitch can be created using the serger and the flatlock stitch to form a threaded gap between two pieces of fabric at the seam. You can weave ribbons or embroidery floss through the threads or leave it plain for a lace effect. If you use a 2-thread setting, the stitches will lie flatter and be less bulky. If your machine won't do a 2-thread setting, the 3-thread setting works just as well. Choose a narrow or wide setting, depending on the ribbons you want to weave through or the size of gap required. For wider stitches, use the left needle and for a narrow finish, use the right needle.

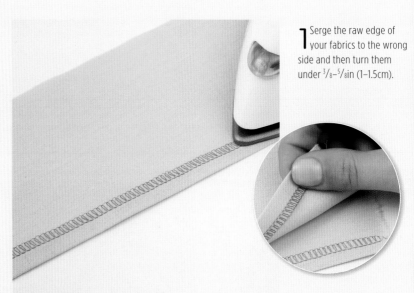

1 Serge the raw edge of your fabrics to the wrong side and then turn them under $\frac{3}{8}$–$\frac{5}{8}$in (1–1.5cm).

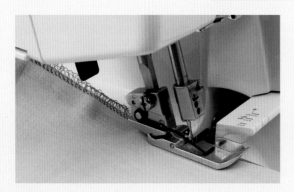

2 Flatlock along the folded edges so that the loops overhang the fold slightly. The more the loops hang over the fold, the wider the gap will be between the fabrics.

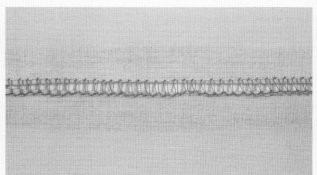

3 Pull open the fabrics and press the stitches flat.

MACHINE SETTINGS
2- or 3-thread flatlocking (using either needle)

Thread tensions
Left needle:	0
Upper looper:	3 (or looser)
Lower looper:	9

Stitch length:	3–4
Stitch width:	Wide setting
Knife:	Deactivated
Foot:	Standard

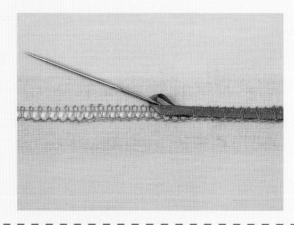

4 Add decoration by weaving through ribbon or embroidery flosses.

Using a piping foot

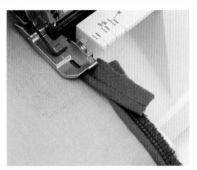

Front of piping foot

Back of piping foot

A piping foot will ensure you get perfectly piped or corded seams. Piping looks great on purses and pillows or used to emphasize seams. Add piping or cord in contrasting colors to accentuate style lines. Adding piping can also strengthen seams and make them more durable. Cover piping cord with bias-cut strips of fabric or use pre-covered cord. On upholstery projects, try this foot with store-bought cord with a flange attached.

WHAT DOES A PIPING FOOT LOOK LIKE?

The piping foot looks similar to the standard foot and may be metal or plastic. The main difference is that the piping foot has a groove underneath to allow the piping to be held in place while sewing. Feet are available with different measurements of groove to suit a range of thicknesses of piping and to work with most models of serger.

HOW DOES IT WORK?

Once the piping foot has been attached, the cording or piping will sit within the groove of the foot, allowing the machine to stitch as close as possible to the piping. This close stitching will ensure that, once the seam is finished, the piping or cording will sit tightly to the edge.

JOINING PIPING

An easy way to join the piping is to overlap. If you are adding piping or cording to a pillow, as you sew back around to the starting point, pull the starting piping tape to one side and lay the end piece on top. Continue to sew, cutting any excess tape away from the starting strip and finishing your piping neatly.

Curves and corners

• To sew around curves, snip several sections of the flange or piping tape.

• To sew around corners, cut the very corner of the piping tape up to the stitch line.

Tips

• Pre-cover and machine baste cord into its cover before stitching it to the fabric.

• Pin the piping or cording in place and then machine or hand baste first to one layer of fabric before completing your sewing on the serger. This is especially worthwhile for slippy or heavy fabrics.

• Always use bias-cut strips if you are covering your own cord. This will allow the cord to go around corners and curves smoothly.

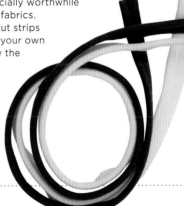

COVERING YOUR OWN PIPING

Covering your own piping is easy. That way, you can match your piping trim exactly to the project you are making. You need to cover the piping cord with strips of fabric cut on the bias. The bias strips will have an amount of stretch to them, allowing you to place your piping around a curve, corner, or shaped edge more easily. The fabric should be cut exactly on a 45-degree angle for a true bias cut. This can seem wasteful at times and so, to save a little bit of fabric or to squeeze a strip onto an offcut of fabric, you can cut the strips at a smaller angle; they will still have some stretch to them.

Tip
The width required for your strips depends on the thickness of the cord you are using. A general rule to cutting strips the right width is to double the width of your cord and double the width of your seam allowance and then add these together. For example, for a $5/8$in (1.5cm) seam allowance and $1/8$in (3mm) cord, the strip would measure $1^1/2$in (4cm).

1 To find the line at 45 degrees, fold your fabric so that the cut edge meets the selvage. Fold or press a crease along this line and then chalk or draw this line onto the fabric.

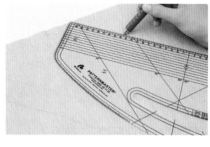

2 Use a ruler to measure the strips and draw these onto the fabric. A quilter's or dressmaker's rule works brilliantly for this.

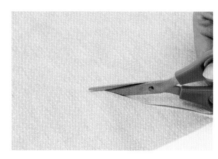

3 Cut the strips out, using long-bladed scissors or a rotary cutter to keep the edges smooth.

4 To piece the strips together, place ends together at right angles and then stitch across using a narrow $1/8$in (3mm) seam allowance. Press the seam allowance flat.

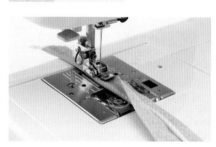

5 Wrap the bias strip around your cord and use a zipper foot to machine baste in place. Don't stitch as close as possible to the piping—leave a gap so that the stitching does not show once the piping is attached to the project.

SERGING WITH A PIPING FOOT

Piping can be inserted either to sit on the edge of the fabric, such as on pillows and seat covers, or in the seam of a garment. The same method and approach can be used for both techniques. The following instructions show how to use self-covered piping, but pre-covered piping or store-bought cord with flange could also be inserted in the same way. You may need to tighten the needle threads to keep all the layers secure.

1 Cut off $3/4$–$1^1/4$in (2–3 cm) from the start of the piping tape or flange.

MACHINE SETTINGS
3- or 4-thread serging (using the left needle for three threads)

Thread tensions	
Left needle:	3
Right needle:	3
Upper looper:	3
Lower looper:	3
Stitch length:	3–4
Stitch width:	Adjust to suit
Knife:	Activated
Foot:	Piping foot

2 Place piping between two layers of fabric—the raw edge should be flush with the edge to be sewn, and the fabric should be right sides together. Pull out the section of tape that has been removed to expose the start point of sewing. Hand or machine baste the piping strip in place to one layer of fabric before serging.

CREATING A LONG LENGTH OF BIAS STRIP

This is an alternative method of creating bias strips (steps 1–4 at left) and allows you to cut one long length much more easily. This is perfect if you need to make a number of yards of fabric to cover pillows or seat pads.

1 Mark out your strips of bias as before and cut a number of strips away from the fabric in one section. Match the edges of the fabric together so that the top of one end aligns with the top of the second strip at the other end.

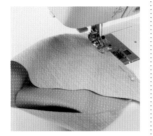

2 Stitch the ends together using a $1/8$in (3mm) seam allowance and form a tube of fabric. Press the seam allowances flat.

3 The bias strips can now be cut in a continuous length.

---

3 Move fabrics forward until they are touching the upper knife. Align the piping under the foot and lower the foot, ensuring the groove is the correct size for the cord and sits comfortably.

4 Begin to sew slowly, guiding the cording into the groove of the foot and keeping all fabric edges together. Your finished seam will look like this, neatly serged. Turn the fabric to the right side; only the edge of the piping should show.

①　②　③　④　⑤　⑥

IDEAS FILE

1. **Piping on a pillow:** Add piping to your pillows to give them more shape and structure. Cut your own bias strips to make your piping match the pillow fabric or use a contrasting fabric to add something different.

2. **Cord around a seat cover:** Use store-bought cord with attached flange and sew into the seam.

3. **Piping on seams of a garment:** Add that professional finish to your homemade garments by adding piping into the seam lines. Use pre-covered store-bought piping to speed up the making process or take the time to cover your own piping in the same or contrasting fabric.

4. **Highlight geometric prints:** Use thicker cord to give your pillow the edge.

5. **Cord on edge of a pocket:** Use a fine upholstery trim to add something special to your pockets—this technique works just as well on hems, necklines, and armholes.

6. **Piping on a skirt:** Place around waistband or yoke in a contrasting color.

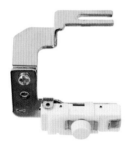

Using an elastic attachment

The elastic attachment, or elasticator, makes sewing on elastic much easier. This little device holds the tension of the elastic, stretching it evenly as you attach it to a fabric edge.

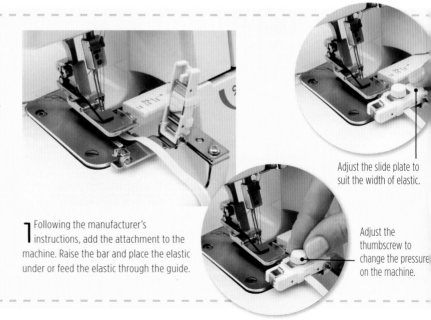

1   2   3

WHAT DOES AN ELASTIC ATTACHMENT FOOT LOOK LIKE?

Most elastic attachments look similar, and may be a foot or an attachement, depending on your serger model. The part of the attachment that sits above the fabric will have a bar running across the top with a slide plate and thumbscrew. Some attachments can take a range of widths of narrow elastics, whereas others have a detachable elastic guide, which comes in different sizes to suit different widths of elastic.

Elastic gathering foot with elastic guides to stitch elastic in a range of widths

HOW DOES IT WORK?

The bar running across the attachment holds the elastic in place and the thumbscrew can be turned to increase or decrease the pressure on the elastic. Increasing the pressure on the elastic will cause it to be more tightly held in place and will result in more gathering on the fabric. Decreasing the pressure on the elastic will mean it is held more loosely and so there will be less gathering on the fabric as the elastic is attached. Adjust the slide plate to accord with the width of elastic being used to ensure that it will be fed straight toward the needles.

Elastic attachment

Types of elastic

Woven: Strong and thick, it is great for heavier-weight fabrics. Can be applied directly to fabrics.

Braided: Gets narrower as it is stretched and may be weakened or lose its stretch if sewn through.

Knitted: Soft, ideal for lightweight fabrics, and can be applied directly to the fabric without weakening or damaging the elastic (1).

Lingerie: Pretty-edged elastic that is ideal for underwear.

Non-roll: Perfect for waistbands as it will stay flat when stretched, making it more comfortable to wear (2).

Cord elastic: Comes in a range of colors and widths. The narrowest can be used for shirring and will fit through the upper looper (3).

Clear elastic: Can stretch up to four times its length while still maintaining its original length when relaxed. Great for applying directly to fabrics for stabilizing shoulders or necklines.

USING THE ELASTIC ATTACHMENT

This attachment will not work on all types of elastic and is best suited to flat elastics with narrow widths. The Janome elastic gathering attachment used here will take elastics from ⅛–⁵⁄₁₆in (3.5–8mm) in width. Other attachments will take slightly wider elastics. The looper cover cannot be opened once this is attached, so make sure your machine is threaded correctly before adding the attachment.

1 Following the manufacturer's instructions, add the attachment to the machine. Raise the bar and place the elastic under or feed the elastic through the guide.

Adjust the slide plate to suit the width of elastic.

Adjust the thumbscrew to change the pressure on the machine.

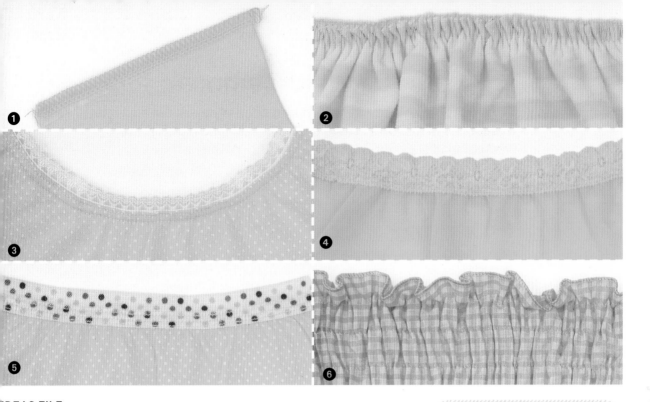

IDEAS FILE

1. **Stabilize shoulder seams:** Use clear elastic on lightweight knitted fabric for stabilizing shoulder seams.
2. **Make a cuff:** Serge narrow elastic to the fabric edge to form a sleeve cuff.
3. **Use lingerie elastic:** Serge in place using the elastic attachment and a narrow stitch, and then topstitch flat using cover stitch.

4. **Decorate lingerie:** Use pretty-edged elastic around the leg and waist openings.
5. **Decorate a skirt:** Attach knitted elastic directly to fabric for a quick unencased waistband on a child's skirt. This wide elastic was applied without using the elastic attachment.
6. **Shirring and smocking:** Cord elastic used in the upper looper works great for shirring or smocking.

Tip
Use a long stitch length when sewing on elastic, as this enables the elastic to recover a better shape. Some types of elastic can be damaged or weakened by too many needle holes.

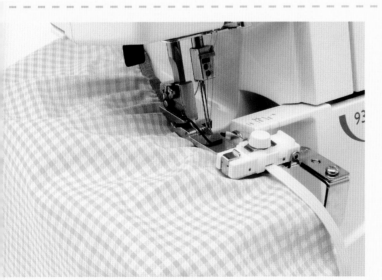

2 Place the fabric under the elastic and under the foot. Begin sewing slowly, making sure the elastic is being attached correctly and the amount of gathering is as desired.

3 Continue to sew to the end of the fabric, cut the elastic, and chain off as normal.

Using a blind hemming foot

A blind hem will provide an invisible or barely visible hem on the right side of the fabric. Using a blind hemming foot will ensure that your hem is sewn straight, so any visible stitches will be even.

WHAT DOES A BLIND HEMMING FOOT LOOK LIKE?
The blind hemming foot has a plastic or metal guide on the side. It is very similar in appearance to the blind hemming foot that is used on a regular sewing machine.

HOW DOES IT WORK?
The guide on the side of the foot is used to help you keep the fabric in the correct position as you sew. Before you begin, adjust the guide so that the fabric fold runs along its edge with the left needle only just catching the folded edge of the fabric.

FABRIC CHOICE
This technique works best on heavier fabrics, such as upholstery fabrics, fleece, and wool fabrics, as the needle can catch a small amount of the fabric more easily without stitching all the way through. It's a really quick finish for hemming curtains instead of having to use a visible straight stitch or sew by hand. It is much more difficult, if not impossible, to use the serger to produce a truly invisible blind hem on medium- and lightweight fabrics because the needles will stitch straight through the fabric, making the threads show on the right side—although this can be used decoratively.

Blind hemming foot

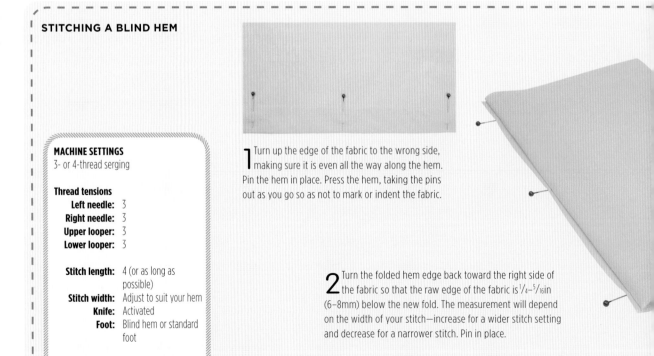

STITCHING A BLIND HEM

MACHINE SETTINGS
3- or 4-thread serging

Thread tensions
Left needle:	3
Right needle:	3
Upper looper:	3
Lower looper:	3

Stitch length:	4 (or as long as possible)
Stitch width:	Adjust to suit your hem
Knife:	Activated
Foot:	Blind hem or standard foot

1 Turn up the edge of the fabric to the wrong side, making sure it is even all the way along the hem. Pin the hem in place. Press the hem, taking the pins out as you go so as not to mark or indent the fabric.

2 Turn the folded hem edge back toward the right side of the fabric so that the raw edge of the fabric is $1/4$–$5/16$in (6–8mm) below the new fold. The measurement will depend on the width of your stitch—increase for a wider stitch setting and decrease for a narrower stitch. Pin in place.

Getting it right

• Stitching a perfect blind hem will require some practice. Test first on scrap fabric to ensure that your finish will be invisible, or as near as possible.

• Use a thread that is the same color or slightly darker than your fabric. This will make any visible stitches less obvious.

• If you find that the stitches are showing, try creating a mock band hem (pages 62–63). Or make a feature of the stitching by creating even stitches that will show on the right side of the fabric. Flatlocking the hem (pages 74–75) is another alternative where the stitches will be seen on the right side of the fabric.

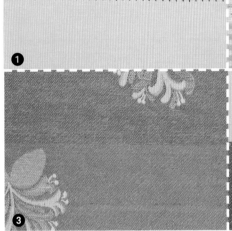

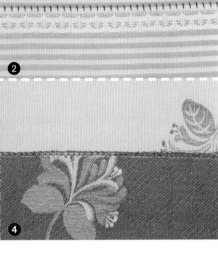

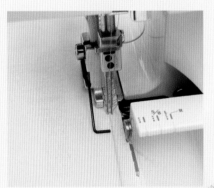

IDEAS FILE

1. **Use contrasting thread:** Make visible stitches into a feature on the hem of cuffs when using a medium- or lightweight fabric.

2. **Apply lace:** Following the instructions below, at step 2 insert a strip of lace to add decoration to the hem of a skirt.

3 & 4. **Blind hem heavy curtains:** Using the blind hem finish on curtains and drapes made from a heavy fabric makes the process quick and easy and gives an almost invisible finish from the right side (3).

4 Sew slowly, making sure that the left needle enters the fabric in the right place. In this picture, the foot has been removed for clarity.

3 Line up your fabric for stitching, with the raw edge nearest the cutting blade. Position the fabric so that the left needle will just skim the fold, sewing only slightly into the fibers on the edge. Don't forget to remove the pins as you sew. The cutting blade will cut off any excess fabric.

Tip
Use the handwheel and turn it toward you and back again so you can see where the needle will enter the fabric. Adjust the guide on the blind hemming foot until the fabric is positioned correctly.

5 When you've finished the seam, chain off, cut the thread, and secure the ends. Open up the fold and lay the fabric flat. Press the hemming stitches flat. You should see only very tiny stitches on the right side of the fabric, or none at all.

Using a gathering foot

You can gather without a gathering foot by adjusting the differential feed to allow one layer of fabric to be gathered at the edge. The gathering foot, however, allows one layer of fabric to be gathered while keeping the other layer flat, as both layers are serged and stitched together.

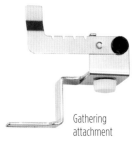

Gathering foot

Gathering attachment

WHAT DOES A GATHERING FOOT LOOK LIKE?

Some machines will have different attachments to allow for gathering one piece of fabric to another. The gathering foot has a raised section that acts as a slot for the top layer of fabric. The gathering attachment has a movable arm that is used to separate the two layers of fabric.

HOW DOES IT WORK?

The slot section on the gathering foot and the arm on the gathering attachment keep the upper layer of fabric separated from the bottom layer and stop the upper layer from touching the front feed dog teeth. The lower layer will be fed into the machine, gathering up as the front feed dog teeth push the fabric toward the rear feed dog teeth. The top layer of fabric is only allowed to touch the rear teeth as it is fed out of the machine, so it does not gather but remains flat as it is attached to the gathered lower layer.

HOW MUCH FABRIC DO I NEED?

If you are gathering using a differential feed set to 2, this means that the ratio is set to 2:1 and that the lower layer will be gathered twice as much as the top. If your bottom piece of fabric is 8in (20cm) long, your top piece should be 4in (10cm) long to fit. If the differential feed is set to 1.5, the bottom layer will be gathered only half as much, so if the bottom layer measures 8in (20cm), the top layer should measure 6in (15cm). This rule does not always work perfectly, because lighter fabrics will gather more and heavier fabrics not as much. Always do a practice test first.

USING THE GATHERING ATTACHMENT

MACHINE SETTINGS
3- or 4-thread serging (using the left needle)

Thread tensions
Left needle:	3
Right needle:	3
Upper looper:	3
Lower looper:	3

Stitch length:	4 (or as long as possible)
Stitch width:	Adjust as necessary
Differential feed:	2 or higher
Knife:	Activated
Foot:	Gathering foot or gathering attachment

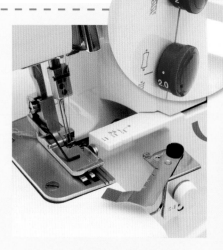

1 Attach the gathering foot to the machine and adjust the differential feed to 2 or higher.

2 Raise the foot and place both layers of fabric underneath. Swing the moveable arm on the gathering attachment so that it separates the two layers of fabric and sits just slightly under the presser foot. If using the gathering foot, place one layer of fabric under the foot and the other layer into the slot on the foot.

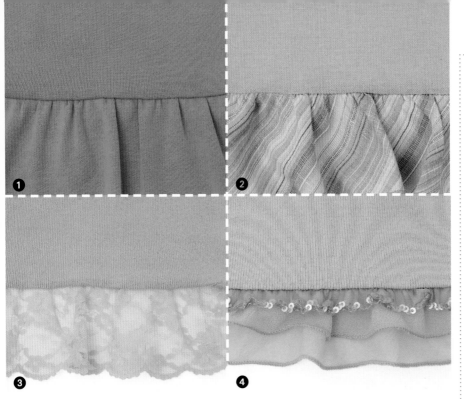

①

②

③

④

GATHERING WITHOUT A FOOT

• If you don't have a gathering foot, adjust the differential feed to 2 and stitch a single layer of fabric. As the fabric is fed through the machine, it should gather along the sewn edge.

• Place this gathered piece right sides together with another layer of fabric. Set the differential feed to 1 and serge again.

IDEAS FILE

1. **Attach a skirt and bodice:** Gather a skirt onto a bodice top quickly and easily with your gathering foot.
2. **Edge soft furnishing:** Make a pretty gathered edge around a pillow or valance in contrasting fabric.

3. **Decorate a sleeve:** Add a gathered lace or sheer fabric cuff to a sleeve.
4. **Two layers of fabric:** Gather two layers of fabric and attach to a skirt or top edge.

3 Lower the foot and begin stitching, keeping the fabric layers separated as you stitch.

4 The finished seam is gathered on one side and remains flat on the other.

Tips

• To adjust the amount of gather, turn the differential feed dial toward 1 or "N" for fewer gathers or up to 2 for more gathers.
• For intermittent gathering along an edge, adjust the differential feed to 1 before sewing the areas you don't want to be gathered.
• If you can't adjust the differential feed, or you want more gathers, adjust the pressure on the presser foot instead. Tighten the pressure for light- and mediumweight fabrics.

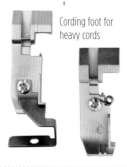

Cording foot for heavy cords

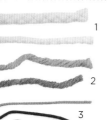

Cording foot for fine cords

Using a cording foot

The cording foot can be used to serge over a range of cords, yarns, and fine wire. Use this foot, combined with a rolled hem, for fine cords or with a narrow hem for thicker yarns to add a decorative or structural edge to your project.

Types of cord

Upholstery or piping cord: May be cotton, nylon, or polyester, and comes in a range of widths and colors (1).

Yarn: Available in a wide range of colors, thicknesses, and fibers, this can give a softer edge to your projects (2).

Waxed cotton cord: Narrow cord used for jewelry making and available in a range of colors and widths—from 0.5mm–2mm (3).

Monofilament thread: Clear thread used for beading or threading. Great for adding an edge to projects or giving definition on garments.

Fishing line: A type of monofilament thread, this is available in different weights for use with light to heavier-weight fabrics (4).

Wire: Craft wire can be found in a range of colors and weights. Choose fine jewelry wire for beading to create a delicate edge, or thicker, less malleable wire for a more defined edge (5).

WHAT DOES A CORDING FOOT LOOK LIKE?

A cording foot has a small hole in the top of the foot, or in a front bar, through which to feed cord. On the underside of the foot, there may be a groove that the cord will sit in as it is being stitched. Some manufacturers make cording feet with a range of different-sized holes, so you can choose the one that will best suit the thickness of cord you are using.

HOW DOES IT WORK?

Cord is inserted through the guide hole and under the groove of the foot. For smaller cording guides, it may be easier to insert the cord before attaching the foot to the machine. As you stitch, the threads will wrap over the cord, creating a decorative edge to a project. The guide hole and groove will ensure that the cord remains in the same position as you sew.

CORDING OVER UPHOLSTERY CORD

This example uses decorative threads in the loopers. For the best thread coverage, keep the stitch length as short as possible.

MACHINE SETTINGS

3-thread roll hemming (using the left needle)

Thread tensions

Left needle:	3
Upper looper:	4
Lower looper:	7
Stitch length:	1 or shorter
Stitch width:	Wide
Knife:	Activated
Foot:	Cording foot

1 Remove the standard foot and attach the cording foot. Lift the presser foot. Insert the cord through the guide hole and through the groove under the foot toward the back of the machine.

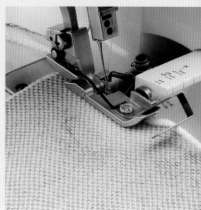

2 Place the fabric under the foot and under the cord. As you stitch, the knife will cut off just the fraying edge of the fabric.

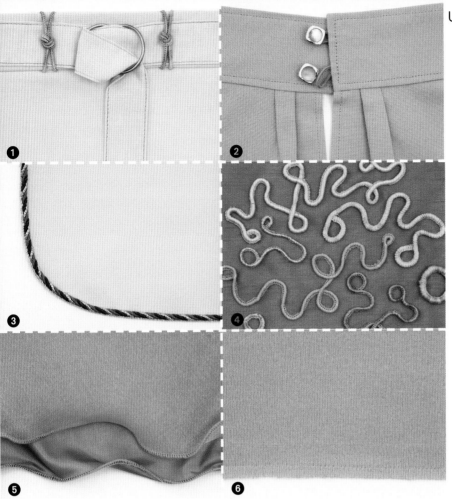

IDEAS FILE

1. **Make belt loops:** Use decorative threads and a rolled hem setting to serge over cords and create a feature of your belt loops. Tie two lengths of cording together for a decorative effect.

2. **Create button loops:** Serge over narrow cord or elastic to create button loops in a contrasting or matching color.

3. **Make a corded edge for placemats or table linen:** Monofilament polyester is ideal for adding a corded edge to your projects, as the colorful cord can be seen through the stitches.

4. **Embellish fabric:** Serge over cord in different threads and then hand sew this in place.

5. **Use fishing line:** To create more volume In the hem of a dress, serge over fishing line.

6. **Reinforce the hem edge:** Use monofilament yarn and a regular 4-thread serging stitch to reinforce the hem edge of knitwear.

Tips

• For decorative cording with more flexible cord, set the thread tensions to the neutral position and use a narrow hem with a medium stitch length between 2 and 4.

• For heavier cord, use a wide rolled hem and the left needle.

• Try wrapping fishing line around a wooden cotton spool and then boiling it for a short time. Once it has cooled, the line can be serged as before but will form more curls in the hem.

• Depending on your type of machine and the accessories available, it may be easier to attach very heavy cords using the beading foot.

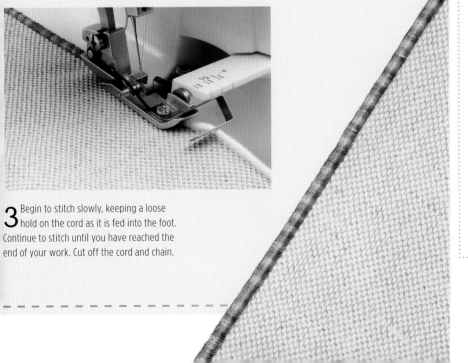

3 Begin to stitch slowly, keeping a loose hold on the cord as it is fed into the foot. Continue to stitch until you have reached the end of your work. Cut off the cord and chain.

Using a bias binding foot

Bias binding can be wrapped over the edge of fabric to add a decorative trim to seams and hems. With a bias binding foot the job is made much quicker and easier, because it allows you to wrap and stitch perfectly in one go. Two general types of feet or attachments are available: one for pre-folded bias tape and one that will fold the tape for you.

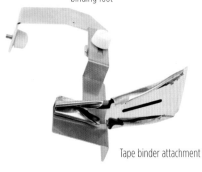

Adjustable bias binding foot

Tape binder attachment

WHAT DOES A BIAS BINDING FOOT LOOK LIKE?

Most bias binding feet have a funnel section at the front through which you can pass bias strips. These will be folded as they are fed through. Other feet may have a smaller opening or a movable guide so that different widths of pre-folded bias tape can be used with the same foot.

HOW DOES IT WORK?

Bias tape or strips are fed into the foot. The foot folds and neatly encases the fabric edge with the bias tape, aligning it perfectly to be stitched correctly into place. Different feet are suitable for either pre-folded or unfolded bias strips.

Tip
Use the cover stitch or top cover stitch to work more lines of stitching on the bias strip.

USING A TAPE BINDER ATTACHMENT

This attachment is used to fold and attach home-cut bias strips.

MACHINE SETTINGS:
2-thread chain stitch (using one of the far left needles) on a multifunctional machine

Thread tensions	
Left needle:	Neutral
Chain looper:	Neutral
Stitch length:	3 (or longer as desired)
Stitch width:	N/A
Knife:	Disengaged
Foot:	Tape binder attachment

1 Cut bias strips 1½in (4cm) wide. Stitch strips together if necessary to form a longer strip (see page 80). Cut one end of the bias strip at a 45-degree angle and insert this into the binder, with the wrong side of the fabric facing outward. Pull the strip through the binder.

USING A BIAS BINDING FOOT

This foot is used to attach pre-folded bias tape. This type of foot can be used for bias tapes with widths from ½–1½in (1–4cm).

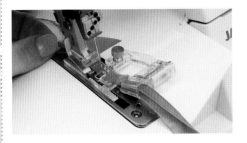

1 Cut one end of the bias tape to a 45-degree angle and insert this into the slot at the front of the foot. Pull the tape under the foot and toward the back of the machine.

2 Adjust the front screw on the foot until the folded edges of the bias tape are lightly touching the edges of the foot.

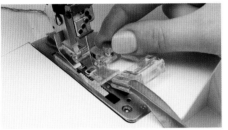

3 Insert the needle into the bias tape, making sure that it is correctly positioned with only $1/16$in (2mm) showing to the left of the needle. Adjust the rear foot screw until the needle is correctly aligned.

4 Line up the fabric, inserting the edge into the folds of the bias binding. Turn the flywheel to start stitching and then continue sewing slowly, using the foot pedal.

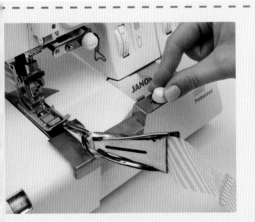

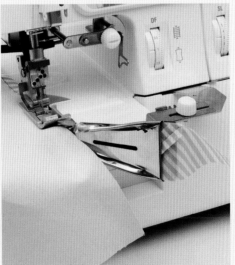

3 Line the fabric up to the bias tape, sliding the edge between the folds of the bias binding. Lower the foot and turn the flywheel toward you to ensure stitches are being made in the right place. Continue stitching slowly until you have competed your edging.

2 Lower the needle into the bias tape, repositioning the binder until only $1/16$in (2mm) of fabric is showing to the left of the needle.

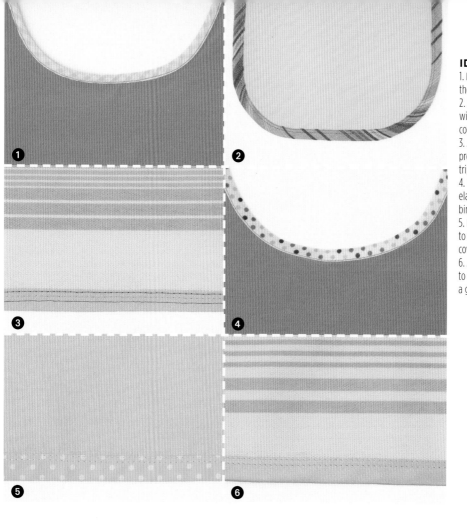

IDEAS FILE

1. **Decorate a T-shirt:** Use bias binding along the neckline and finish with chain stitch.
2. **Decorate a placemat**: Finish the edges with contrasting homemade binding and cover stitch.
3. **Add interest to a hem:** Bind a hem with pre-folded, store-bought binding, using the triple cover stitch and decorative threads.
4. **Work with elastic:** Attach fold-over elastic to an edge more easily using the bias binding foot.
5. **Finish a sleeve:** Attach contrasting binding to the edge of a sleeve and finish using the cover stitch.
6. **Add a shimmer:** Use satin bias binding to add a touch of shimmer to the edges of a garment.

MAKING YOUR OWN BIAS BINDING STRIPS

It is easy to make your own bias strips. Cut them just under twice as wide as the binding you require. See page 80 for more information on cutting strips. To fold your own bias strip, use a bias trim maker—a neat little gadget that will fold your strips for you.

Cut your bias strips. Feed the strip through the bias trim maker. As the fabric comes out the end of the bias trim maker, press it flat so that it stays folded.

Using a taping foot

This foot enables you to attach ribbon, braid, and seam tape. It keeps the tape in the right position as you sew, making serging much easier. Try using different stitches with the taping foot for varied effects.

Standard foot with tape slit

1 **2** **3** **4**

WHAT DOES A TAPING FOOT LOOK LIKE?

A taping foot has a slit to one side or in the middle of the foot. For some brands, the standard foot that comes with the serger will have this feature, making it multipurpose for a range of different uses. Some machines have an added taping attachment, which has an arm and reel for holding larger quantities of tape.

HOW DOES IT WORK?

Ribbon or tape is fed through the slit in the foot and then under the foot toward the back. The foot keeps the ribbon in position as it is sewn, correctly lining it up under the needles. For longer strips of tape, the taping attachment can be used. Wind the tape onto the reel before attaching it to the machine.

IDEAS FILE

1. **Add interest to a skirt hem:** Attach ribbon and lace using cover stitch.
2. **Decorate a garment edge:** Attach a ribbon using chain stitch. The straight stitch is seen from the right side of garment and the chain from underneath.
3. **Make decorative braid:** Use a top cover stitch and decorative thread to stitch over twill tape. Use these as braids or belt loops.
4. **Secure shoulder seams:** Attach narrow twill tape with a 4-thread serging stitch to keep shoulder seams secure.

USING THE TAPING FOOT

This taping foot from Janome can be used for tape widths of 1/8–5/16in (4–8mm). Cover stitch is used here, but any stitch can be used with this foot.

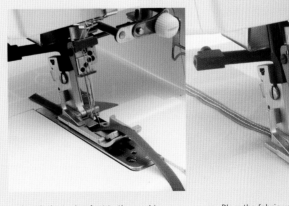

1 Attach the taping foot to the machine. Pass the tape through the slit on the foot and then under the foot and toward the back of the machine.

2 Place the fabric under the foot and lower the foot. Wind the handwheel toward you and into the tape and fabric. Pull some slack on the tape and then begin sewing slowly, guiding the tape slightly with your fingers as you stitch.

Using a beading attachment

Strings of beads, sequins, and heavier cord can be attached to fabrics using the beading attachment—great for embellishing bridal or evening wear to give a stunning finish to a garment.

WHAT DOES A BEADING ATTACHMENT LOOK LIKE?
This type of foot has a groove underneath and sometimes one on the top also, for feeding beads through.

Beading attachment

HOW DOES IT WORK?
Place a string of beads or heavy cord in the groove on top of the foot and then into the groove under the foot. These grooves keep the beads in the correct position so that, as you stitch, the beads are attached evenly to the fabric.

Beading foot for use with attachment

Clear beading foot

Tip
Use a monofilament thread so that the stitching is barely visible on the fabric.

USING THE BEADING ATTACHMENT
This Janome beading attachment can be used for beads from 1–4mm in width. The beads do not have to be placed on the hem edge of the fabric; you can attach them to a folded edge so that they can be used anywhere on the fabric.

MACHINE SETTINGS
2- or 3-thread flatlocking (using the left needle)

Thread tensions
Left needle:	1
Upper looper:	3
Lower looper:	7

Stitch length:	3–4 or longer
Stitch width:	Wide
Knife:	Deactivated
Foot:	Beading foot

1 Set the machine up for flatlocking using the left needle and then deactivate the cutting knife. Remove the standard foot and attach the beading foot and attachment.

2 Lift the presser foot. Insert the beads through the groove of the attachment and under the groove of the foot toward the back of the machine.

3 Lower the foot. Begin stitching, using the handwheel for two to three stitches to secure the beads to the thread chain. Adjust the stitch length so that each stitch catches a bead.

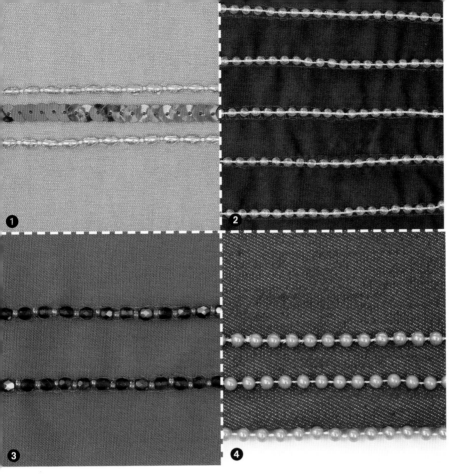

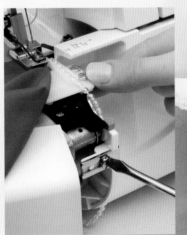

IDEAS FILE

1. **Attach sequins:** Use the beading foot and clear thread.
2. **Create a purse:** Attach clear beads along a number of rows.
3. **Rows of beading:** Sew beads (two or three rows) across the top edge of an evening dress.
4. **Decorate a hem:** Bead along the hemline of a dress.

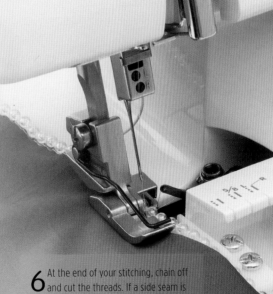

4 Fold the fabric with the wrong sides together. Place it under the foot so that the fold sits next to the beads.

5 Turn the handwheel and adjust the beading guide by loosening the attaching screw. Position the foot so that the needle just catches the edge of the fold. Lower the foot and begin to stitch slowly.

6 At the end of your stitching, chain off and cut the threads. If a side seam is to be sewn, remove any beads that would be in the way of this. Tie off the thread ends and cut.

CHAPTER 3
Quick Constructions

By now you'll have realized that there's a whole host of things that you can achieve with your serger, and the projects in this chapter will give you a chance to experiment and expand your skills further. These projects are all designed to be easily achievable with the skills you've learned so far and will show you that you can use your serger to create impressive garments, accessories, and homewares without complicated patterns or spending hours at the sewing machine.

Evening scarf/beach cover-up

This is the quickest and easiest of all the projects, but it can be made to look like an expensive purchase if you use the right decorative threads. Made from a rectangle of chiffon fabric, the scarf is roll hemmed on all sides using contrasting or matching decorative threads. Use a metallic or silky thread for interest or a woolly polyester thread for better coverage. Change the fabric to lightweight cotton and this project can be transformed into a cover-up for the beach.

YOU WILL NEED
- ½yd (0.5m) chiffon, or approximately 2yd (2m) lightweight cotton
- 2 spools matching thread (polyester or polycotton)
- 1 spool decorative thread for upper looper
- fabric scissors
- washable fabric marker or chalk
- tape measure
- bodkin

Cutting out the fabric
- For a scarf, cut a rectangle ½yd (0.5m) x the width of your fabric.
- For a beach cover-up, cut a rectangle 2yd (2m) x the width of your fabric.

Adjust the size of fabric to suit your preferences.

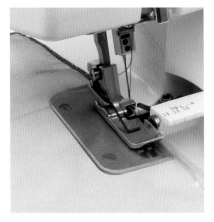

1 Set up your machine for roll hemming—2-thread if you have it, or 3-thread if not. Use the decorative thread in the upper looper.

Look elegant in your own decoratively serged scarf—a perfect first project for roll hemming on your serger.

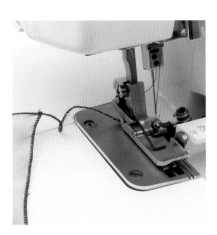

2 Serge around the sides of the rectangle, cutting off only the fraying edge and using the continuous stitching method (see page 52).

3 Secure the remaining chain end by threading onto a bodkin or large-eyed needle and burying into the stitching.

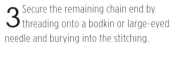

Simple top

This easy slouch top can be made within an hour! Seams are formed with a 4-thread serging stitch and the lower edge is finished with a mock band hem. Fabric bands are added to the armholes and neckline. The possibilities are endless with this simple shape—add contrasting armhole bands and cut out a separate lower band to make your top different.

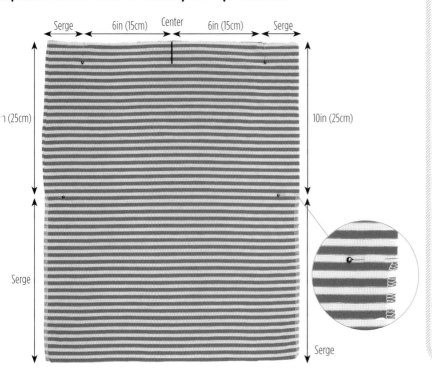

YOU WILL NEED
- 1yd (1m) or more lightweight jersey t-shirt fabric
- 4 spools matching thread (polyester or polycotton)
- fabric scissors
- washable fabric marker or chalk
- ruler or tape measure
- pins
- iron

Optional
20in (50cm) contrasting fabric to form armhole bands and collar

Cutting out the fabric
- Measure around your bust, halve this measurement, and then add 1in (2.5cm). This will be the width measurement.
- Measure from your shoulder to your hip. This will be the length measurement.
- Cut 2 rectangles width measurement x length.
- Cut 2 rectangles 20 x 2½in (50 x 6cm) for the armhole bands.
- Cut 1 rectangle 23½ x 12in (60cm x 30cm) for the collar.

If a longer top or dress is required, add additional length when you cut out the fabric.

Optional
For contrasting lower edge band, cut 2 rectangles width measurement x 3in (8cm). Adjust length of top to allow for this new lower band by taking off 1¼in (3cm).

1 Place the two larger rectangles right sides together. Measure 10in (25cm) from the top edge on each side down the length of the rectangle and place a marker.

2 Find the center of the width of the rectangle and place a marker. Measure 6in (15cm) from each side of this marker and mark this.

3 Using 4 threads, serge from the bottom edge of the rectangle to the marker on each side seam. Serge across the width from each end to the markers near the center. Press seams flat.

4 Create a mock band hem at the bottom edge of the top by turning up the raw edge to the inside of the garment by 1½in (4cm) and following the instructions on pages 62–63.

ATTACHING THE ARMHOLE BANDS

5 Fold each armhole band right sides together so the shorter ends meet. Serge across these short ends and press the seams flat.

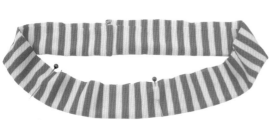

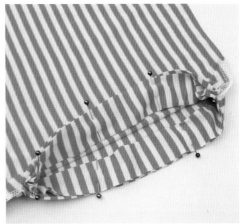

6 Fold the armhole band with wrong sides together and pin so that the raw edges meet.

7 Pin the armhole band right sides together to the garment, centering the seam over the side seam of the garment and stretching to fit where necessary.

8 Start near the side seam and serge the armhole band in place. Press the seam flat toward the inside of the top.

9 Fold the collar right sides together so that the shorter ends meet. Serge across the end.

10 Fold the collar with wrong sides together and pin so that the raw edges meet. Fold the collar in half and half again to mark the center opposite the seam and the quarter points.

11 Find the center of the back and front neckline on the top by folding shoulder seam to shoulder seam—mark these center points.

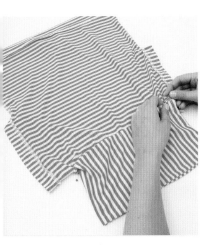

12 With right sides together, pin the collar to the neckline, matching the seam on the collar to the center back on the garment, and the other markers to the center front and side seams of the garment. You may need to stretch slightly to fit, as no seam allowance was added to the collar.

13 Start near the center back and serge around the neck edge of the garment. Press the seam toward the inside of the top.

ADDING A CONTRASTING LOWER BAND

14 To add a contrasting lower band instead of the mock band hem, omit step 4. Serge the two contrasting rectangles together at the shortest edge to form a continuous strip of fabric. Press the seams flat and fold wrong sides together so that the raw edges meet. Attach in the same way as the collar, matching seams to side seams.

Try taking a measurement from your shoulder to the floor to make this quick, simple top into a dress (use the larger of your hip or bust measurement for the width). For winter, use a thick, stretch jersey fabric.

Tote bag

This tote bag is one of the easiest projects to make. It is constructed from rectangles of fabric, serged to make the seams of the bag, and stitched on the sewing machine to create the hems and to attach the handles.

1 Place the two rectangles right sides together and pin.

2 Serge across three of the sides, using a 4-thread stitch and $^1/_2$in (1cm) seam allowance. (Only a tiny amount of fabric will be trimmed off.) Keep one of the shorter sides open.

YOU WILL NEED
- $^1/_2$yd (0.5m) medium- to heavyweight cotton fabric
- 4 spools matching thread (polyester or polycotton)
- fabric scissors
- washable fabric marker or chalk to mark out rectangles
- ruler or tape measure
- pins
- iron

Cutting out the fabric
- Cut 2 rectangles 20 x 14$^1/_2$in (50 x 37cm) for the main part of the bag.
- Cut 2 strips of fabric 27$^1/_2$ x 3in (70 x 7cm) for the handles.

Finished bag measures approximately 17 x 14in (43 x 35cm)

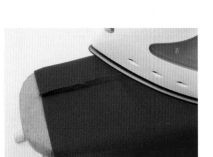

3 Press the seams to one side. Turn the bag right side out.

4 To form the hem on the open edge, turn under 2in (5cm) to the wrong side all the way along, pin, and press a crease into the fabric.

5 Take out the pins and turn the raw edge in to meet the crease, folding the fabric over again along the crease. Pin in place.

6 Using the sewing machine and a straight stitch, stitch close to the inner folded edge. Press the hem flat.

MAKING THE HANDLES

7 To make handles, fold the strips right sides together along the longest edge. Pin in place. Serge, taking out the pins as you go.

Tip
These instructions are kept very simple, but you can add ribbon to the seams (see pages 60–61), use decorative threads (see page 76–78), or adjust the measurements of the bag and handles to suit you.

8 Turn the handles right sides out using a loop turner, or by threading the serged chain through the eye of a blunt needle and feeding this through the handle. As the needle is pulled through, the fabric will turn right side out.

Quick and easy to make, this is the perfect companion on any shopping trip and can be folded up to fit in your purse. A heavyweight fabric will add durability and strength.

9 Turn the raw edges under to one side on each end by 1in (2.5cm).

10 Pin the handles in place to the inside of the bag, 3¹/₂in (9cm) from the sides. Place the handles so that the folded-under raw edge will be hidden once stitched. Stitch in place using the sewing machine. Stitch in a square and then across the diagonals to add extra strength.

Child's dress

Make this pretty little dress quickly and easily on the serger. Made in lightweight cotton, this is ideal for summer. Create a shirred top using elastic in the looper of your machine and a chain stitch setting. A serged French seam is used at the back of the dress to add strength to the garment and to ensure that the shirring elastic stays in place. Make four quick straps to attach to the top of the dress—these are tied in a bow on the shoulder.

> **Tip**
> This project uses chain stitch with shirring elastic in the looper. Don't worry if you can't do a chain stitch on your serger—mark the chalk lines on the wrong side of the fabric, fold along them, and set your machine to 2- or 3-thread flatlocking using the shirring elastic in the upper looper (see page 74). Stitch along the folded edge so that the needle just catches the edge as you stitch.

YOU WILL NEED
- 1/2yd (0.5m) lightweight cotton fabric
- matching thread (polyester or polycotton)
- decorative thread for roll hemming
- fabric scissors
- 9yd (8m) shirring elastic (matching color if possible)
- washable fabric marker or chalk
- ruler or tape measure
- pins
- iron

Cutting out the fabric
- Cut 1 rectangle 39 x 16in (100 x 40cm).
- Cut 2 strips of fabric 28 x 1½in (72 x 4cm).

This dress will fit a child aged 2–5 years, but can easily be made bigger or smaller depending on the size needed.

1 Using a washable fabric marker or chalk, on the right side of the fabric, draw seven lines ³⁄₈in (1cm) apart near one long edge. If using the roll hemming method, draw these lines on the wrong side of the fabric.

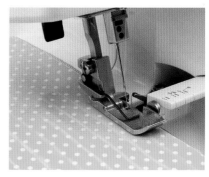

2 Set your machine to roll hemming, with the decorative thread in the upper looper and polyester thread in the lower looper and needles. Serge the top and bottom edges of the dress (the longest sides of your rectangle).

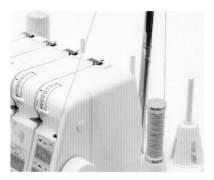

3 Set your machine to chain stitch. Thread shirring elastic through the looper and use polyester thread in the needle. Loosen the tension on the needle and slightly tighten the tension on the looper.

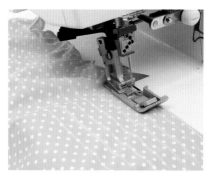

4 Test the shirring on scrap fabric to make sure that the tensions are correct. Stitch across the lines marked on the fabric. Fasten ends of rows by knotting to stop the chain from raveling. Make sure you have a long tail end of elastic at the end of the row or the elastic will spring back into the machine and you will need to rethread the looper.

5 Change the settings on the machine to standard 3-thread serging with the right needle. To create the serged French seam, begin with the wrong sides of the fabric together and serge the back seam, encasing the elastic knots.

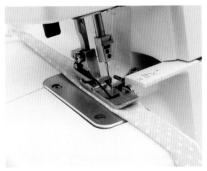

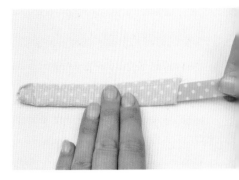

6 Change your machine settings to 4-thread serging and stitch again, giving the back seam more strength and keeping the elastic ends secured. Press the seam.

MAKE THE STRAPS

7 Fold a strap in half with right sides together along the longest edge. Serge across the three raw edges.

8 Cut the strip in half, so that you now have two straps. Turn each piece right side out. Repeat steps 6 and 7 to make another two straps.

9 Lay the dress flat, centering the seam at the back. Pin the straps to the top edge of the dress, 2$\frac{1}{2}$in (6cm) from the center on front and back.

10 Attach the straps to the top edge of the dress, using the sewing machine or hand stitching, turning in the raw edge and fixing with a few stitches.

Show off your shirring skills! This dress is perfect for summer and really simple to make.

Quick quilt

This quilt is made by stitching the cotton batting and fabric all in one go, so there is no need for additional quilting stitches afterward. Five mediumweight cotton fabrics are used to create the main part of the quilt. One of these fabrics is used to create the backing. The edging is applied using homemade binding strips. Due to the thickness of the quilt, these are attached with a sewing machine and hand finished. Since the binding will be attached to straight edges this does not need to be cut on the bias, saving you lots of fabric.

 Fabric A

 Fabric B

 Fabric C

 Fabric D

 Fabric E

YOU WILL NEED

- 12in (30cm) different fabrics for the center strips (Fabrics A, B, C, and D)
- 24in (60cm) fabric for the top and bottom strip of the quilt (Fabric E)
- 69in (1.75m) fabric for the back of the quilt (Fabric C)
- 69in (1.75m) cotton batting
- 4yd (4.25m) single-fold bias binding 1–2in (2.5–5cm) wide
- 4 spools contrasting thread (polyester or polycotton)
- fabric scissors or rotary cutter
- washable fabric marker or chalk
- ruler or quilter's ruler
- tape measure
- long pins or quilter's clips
- iron

Cutting out the fabric

Fabric and batting will be cut into strips measuring 10½ x 40in (27 x 102cm).

- Cut 7 strips of fabric C (1 for the front, 6 for the back of the quilt).
- Cut 2 strips of fabric E.
- Cut 1 strip each of fabrics A, B, and D.
- Cut 6 strips of batting.

Finished quilt measures approximately 59 x 39½in (1.5 x 1m).

The measurements given will allow for some inaccuracy in the cutting of fabric by the store, which means that you will have a tiny bit left over once you cut out your carefully measured pieces.

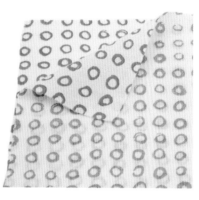

1 Place two strips of fabric C right sides together.

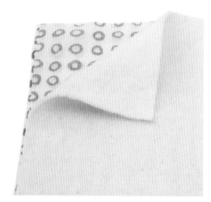

2 Place a strip of batting on top.

3 Place a strip of fabric A right side up on top of the batting.

4 Place a strip of fabric E on top, right side down.

5 Place a strip of batting on top of this.

6 Pin these strips together so that the pins are parallel to the edge but far enough in not to get caught in the serger.

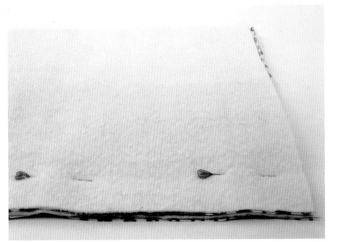

7 Serge through all thicknesses, trimming off a small amount of fabric to keep a $\frac{1}{2}$-in (1-cm) seam allowance.

8 Open out the fabric so you now see the right sides of A and E on one side and the right sides of two fabric C strips on the other side. The batting should be sandwiched in between. Press this seam flat from both sides of the quilt.

9 On the right side of the quilt, place one strip of fabric B right side down on fabric A.

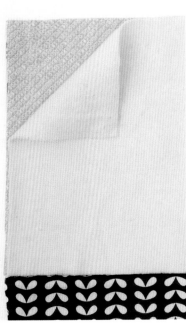

10 Place a strip of batting on top.

11 On the underside of the quilt, place a strip of fabric C right side down.

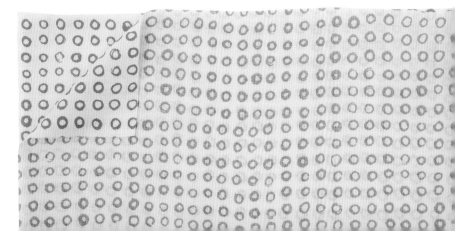

12 Pin together and serge through all thicknesses with a $^1/_2$-in (1-cm) seam allowance.

13 Open out the batting and fabric B on the right side of the quilt. Press the seam flat.

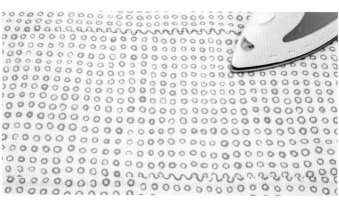

14 Turn the quilt over and open out strip C. Press the seam flat.

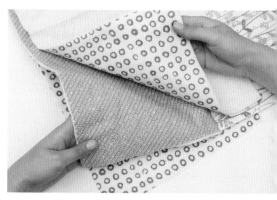

15 Place a strip of fabric C right sides together with fabric B. Place a strip of batting on top. Place a strip of fabric C right sides together with fabric C on the underside of the quilt. Pin and serge together as before.

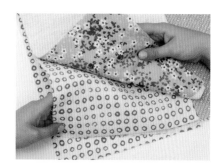

16 Place a strip of fabric D right sides together with fabric C. Place a strip of batting on top. Place a strip of fabric C right sides together with fabric C on the underside of the quilt. Pin and serge together. Open out the fabrics and press the seams flat on both sides.

17 Place the final strip E right sides together with fabric D. Place a strip of batting on top and a strip of fabric C right sides together with fabric C on the underside. Pin in place and serge. Open out the fabrics and press the seams flat on both sides. Your quilt is now ready for binding.

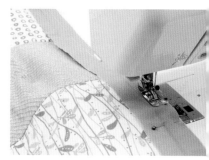

18 Trim the edges of the quilt to even up the fabric layers. Prepare your binding strips by stitching together as necessary and folding through the center. Start with the longest edge and pin the binding right sides together to the quilt, keeping the raw edges even and leaving $^5/_8$in (1.5cm) overhanging at the start end. Machine stitch in place with a $^1/_2$-in (1.3cm) seam allowance.

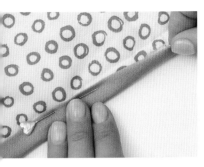

19 Fold the binding over to the underside of the quilt, enclosing the raw edges of the fabric. Turn the raw edge of the binding in and pin in place.

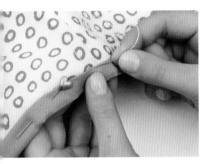

20 Slipstitch the binding in place, stitching through the folds of the binding and into the fabric of the quilt. This should give an almost invisible finish.

21 Attach the binding to the shorter sides of the quilt. Finish the corners by folding in the raw edge to sit flush with the longest edge and folding in the binding as before. Pin in place and finish using slipstitch.

Snuggle up under this quilt on a cold evening or use it to lie out on the grass for a summer picnic.

Pillow cover

This is a quick and easy way to make a pillow cover—no need for zippers, buttons, or buttonholes to keep it closed. Just pull the back opening shut with the ties. This is a great way to store the quilt (see page 106) when you're not using it to snuggle into. You can adjust the size of your pillow cover and adapt the cutting-out instructions at right.

(see page 106)

YOU WILL NEED
- ¹/₂yd (0.5m) medium- to heavyweight fabric
- 4 spools matching thread
- fabric scissors
- washable fabric marker or chalk
- ruler or tape measure
- pins
- iron

Cutting out the fabric
- Cut 1 square 20 x 20in (50 x 50cm).
- Cut 2 rectangles 20 x 10⁵/₈in (50 x 26cm)— width of square x half of square + 1¹/₈in (3cm).
- For the ties cut 1 rectangle 1¹/₂ x 27¹/₂in (4 x 70cm).

Finished pillow cover measures approximately 19 x 19in (48 x 48cm).

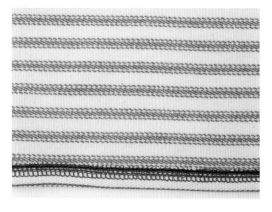

1 Hem one long side of each rectangle. This can be done by cover stitch, flatlock hem, blind hem, serging and then stitching on the sewing machine, or by creating a rolled hem. Here, the pillow cover is serged and then folded over and stitched again on the sewing machine.

MAKE THE TIES

2 Set the machine for 4-thread serging and chain a length of thread 1yd (1m) long.

3 Wrap the chain by folding the long thin rectangle in two along the longest edge, enclosing the chain of thread.

4 Stitch along the edge, making sure that the thread chain is not caught up inside.

5 Pull on the serged chain inside the strip of fabric. This will pull the tie right side out. If it doesn't work, use a loop turner to pull it right side out.

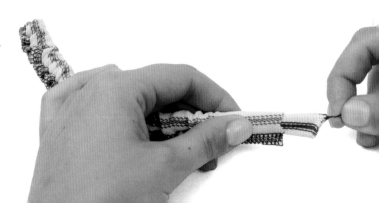

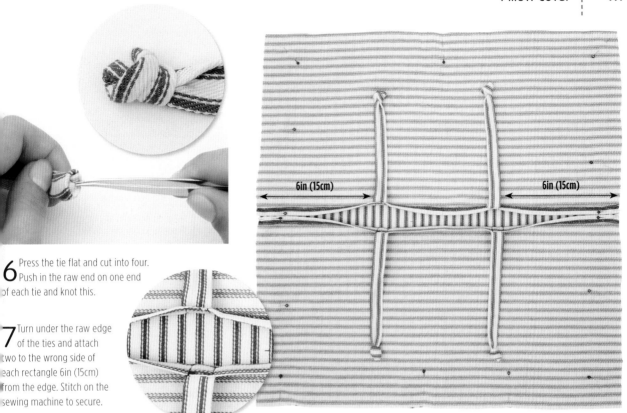

6 Press the tie flat and cut into four. Push in the raw end on one end of each tie and knot this.

7 Turn under the raw edge of the ties and attach two to the wrong side of each rectangle 6in (15cm) from the edge. Stitch on the sewing machine to secure.

8 Place the unhemmed edge of one rectangle on one side of the square right sides together. Place the other rectangle along the opposite edge of the square right sides together. Pin in place.

9 Serge across all four sides, keeping the ties out of the way. Turn right side out and press flat.

Using upholstery fabric such as this blue ticking fabric makes this pillow cover robust and sturdy. You can use it for storing blankets or quilts when they're not in use.

Drawstring bag

To make this drawstring bag or backpack, you use a serger only, so it is a really quick project. Made with mediumweight cotton, it would be great as a shoe bag, child's sport kit bag, or handy day bag. Use a heavier upholstery fabric to make a stronger, more durable bag for carrying heavier items.

YOU WILL NEED
- 20in (50cm) medium- or heavyweight fabric 45in (114cm) wide
- 4 spools matching thread (polycotton or polyester)
- 1 spool decorative thread (optional)
- fabric scissors
- washable fabric marker or chalk
- ruler or tape measure
- pins
- iron
- safety pin or bodkin

Cutting out the fabric
- Cut 1 rectangle 14½ x 33in (37 x 84cm) for bag.
- Cut 2 strips 39¼ x 1¼in (100 x 3cm) for ties. (If you are using heavyweight fabric, increase the width of the ties to 1½in/4cm. This will make turning them to the right side easier.)

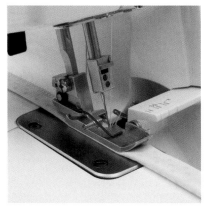

MAKING THE TIES

1 To make the ties, set the machine up for 3-thread serging.

2 Fold one strip widthwise with right sides together, pin in place, and serge the long raw edge and one short edge.

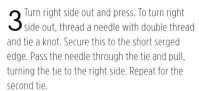

3 Turn right side out and press. To turn right side out, thread a needle with double thread and tie a knot. Secure this to the short serged edge. Pass the needle through the tie and pull, turning the tie to the right side. Repeat for the second tie.

MAKING THE BAG

4 On each long edge of the rectangle, measure 4in (10cm) from each end and mark with chalk.

5 Set the machine to 4-thread serging. Serge from the end of the long edge to the first marker—serging only 4in (10cm) along the edge through a single thickness of fabric.

6 Repeat for the other side and then at the other end of the rectangle. You will have serged four small openings, which will be the openings for the drawstrings.

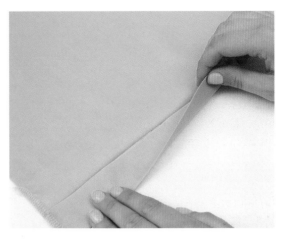

7 Fold each short edge over by 2³/₄in (7cm) to the wrong side. Pin in place and press to form a crease. Unpin and unfold.

8 Turn the raw edge in to meet the fold, and press. Fold over again along the first crease. Pin in place and press again. This will give a guide to sewing the seam that will form the casing for the ties.

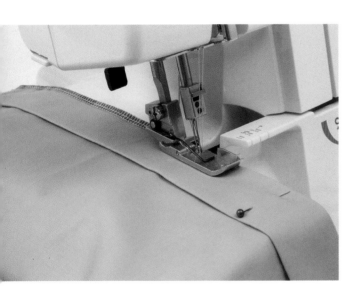

9 Set the machine for 4-thread serging, using decorative thread in the upper looper to make the next seam a feature. (Use ordinary thread if you prefer.) Stitch across the short edge of the fabric, along the fold. Try not to let the blade cut the folded edge (disengage the blade if this is easier).

10 Fold the rectangle in half widthwise, right sides together, so that the finished short edges meet.

11 Serge from the folded edge to the finished edge on each side, stopping as you reach the serged stitches from step 5. Work in the thread ends using a yarn needle to make the seam secure.

12 Press the seams to one side and turn the bag right side out.

13 Use a bodkin or safety pin to thread one tie from the front left side of the bag, through the casing, and out of the right end. Then go across the gap and through the casing on the back.

14 Thread the second tie from the front right side, through the casing, and out of the left side. Then go across the gap and through the casing on the back.

15 On each end of the ties push a little fabric back into the ends and secure with some hand stitches. Secure the tie ends with a simple 2-strand knot.

Turn the page to learn how to make the drawstring backpack variation ▶

These drawstring bags have so much potential and suit a range of different fabrics. Ideal for children's sports kits or shoes; make the measurements smaller to make a drawstring jewelry bag, or scale it up to make a travel laundry bag to keep in your suitcase.

Drawstring backpack

An alternative to the simple drawstring bag, this backpack is perfect for children to take on day trips.

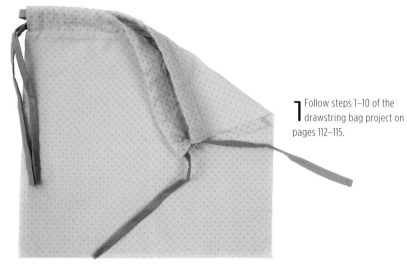

1 Follow steps 1–10 of the drawstring bag project on pages 112–115.

YOU WILL NEED
- 20in (50cm) medium- or heavyweight fabric 45in (114cm) wide
- 3 spools matching thread (polycotton or polyester)
- decorative thread (optional)
- fabric scissors
- washable fabric marker or chalk
- ruler or tape measure
- pins
- iron
- safety pin or bodkin

Cutting out the fabric
- Cut 1 rectangle 14$\frac{1}{2}$ x 33in (37 x 84cm) for bag.
- Cut 2 strips 43$\frac{3}{4}$ x 1$\frac{1}{4}$in (110 x 3cm) for ties. (If you are using heavyweight fabric, increase the width of the ties to 1$\frac{1}{2}$in/4cm. This will make turning them to the right side easier.)

2 Thread the ties through the casing, as described in steps 13 and 14 of the drawstring bag project.

3 On each side of the bag, there are now two ends. Take these ends to the bottom corner on each side of the bag and secure with a pin. Remember to take your pins out before this part of the seam reaches the serger blade.

4 Serge from the folded edge to the finished edge, stopping as you reach the serged stitches from step 5 of the drawstring bag.

5 Work in the thread ends, using a yarn needle to make the seam secure.

6 Press the seam to one side and turn the bag right side out.

Tube skirt

This skirt will look great in any jersey fabric and is surprisingly quick to make. For a warm winter feel try it in a thick heavyweight jersey such as ponte roma, or for a summery feel use a lighter-weight cotton jersey or t-shirt fabric. The pattern is created from rectangular shapes, so it's really simple!

Tip
Make sure you take the pins out of the fabric as you come to sew them—leaving them in will damage the cutting blade!

YOU WILL NEED:
- 1yd (1m) stretch fabric (more for a longer skirt)
- 4 spools matching thread (polyester or polycotton)
- 1yd (1m) of 1in (2.5cm) wide elastic
- fabric scissors
- washable fabric marker or chalk
- ruler
- tape measure
- pins
- iron
- safety pin

Cutting out the fabric:
- For the fabric width, measure around your hips and then halve this measurement.
- For the fabric length, measure from your waist to where you want the skirt to come (eg. above/to/below the knee). Add 1³/₈in (3.5cm) to this measurement for hemming and seam allowances.
- Cut 2 rectangles of fabric using these two measurements for length and width.

Make sure that the stretchiest part of the fabric is across the width/hip measurement.

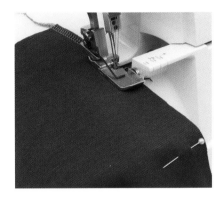

1 Lay the two skirt pieces right side together and pin the side edges. Serge these edges together, trimming off just the fraying edge.

2 Press the seam allowances toward the back of the skirt and turn the skirt to the right side. Try on the skirt. Take the side seams in by stitching them again and cutting off your serged seam (and some of the fabric edge if necessary) to create a closer fit.

3 Place the elastic around your waist and overlap the ends until you are happy with the fit. If you are making the skirt for someone else, the elastic should measure 3–5in (7.5–12.5cm) less than the waist measurement. Overlap the ends of the elastic and stitch to form a circle, using the zigzag setting on your sewing machine.

4 Fold the elastic circle in half and in half again. Mark the folded sections with a fabric marker or chalk, so that the piece is now marked into quarters. Repeat this step with the skirt.

5 Match the elastic seam to one of the side seams on the inside of the skirt. Pin the elastic in place, roughly matching the quarter markers on the skirt to those on the elastic. These won't line up exactly at this point, as you'll find that the elastic is slightly shorter than the fabric.

6 Serge the elastic in place, trimming only the fabric, not the elastic. Stretch the elastic as you stitch, pulling behind and in front of the needles so as not to put undue stress on the needles.

7 Fold the top of the skirt over, encasing the elastic to create a waistband. Pin in place.

Tips
• Use a longer length of fabric and make a maxi-length skirt to the floor. Cozy and warm for winter or cool for the summer.
• Use your bust measurement instead of your hip measurement and create a tube top. Lengthen this top to create a dress.
• No need to add shaping for your curves—stretch fabric will stretch to fit you perfectly. If you want a more snug fit, just take in the side seams a bit more.

8 Use a cover stitch to stitch the elastic in place, stretching the elastic so that the fabric sits flat as you stitch. The stitching should catch the edge of the elastic. Stretch the elastic in front of and behind the needles to minimize pressure on the needles, which could cause them to break. Alternatively, the sewing machine could be used with a straight stitch or narrow zigzag.

9 Hem the lower edge of the skirt using a cover stitch, blind hem, mock band hem, serge and stitch, or just serging alone. Put on your skirt and wear it with pride!

These garments are so versatile and so easy to make that you'll soon have one in every color. Dress it up or down and make it wearable for any occasion.

Guide to fabrics

This section gives guidance on how to get the most from your machine when working with different fabrics. It suggests settings for differential feed and stitch length and also gives details on the correct needle size to use, as well as providing additional notes on seam and hemming techniques to use for the best results.

The serger can tackle almost all types of fabrics. When sewing seams or edge finishing, a serger will be simpler to use than a sewing machine and will yield better results for most fabrics. Knowing the correct settings, needles, and threads to use on your machine will enable you to sew perfect seams and hems.

With so many different types of fabrics available, it is not possible to list every single one. This guide has three generic categories: each category includes a selection of fabrics and gives serger settings and helpful tips.

There are many different threads that can be used for each type of fabric. Generally, stronger threads will be needed for heavier fabrics and lightweight threads for lighter fabrics. However, depending on the chosen project or edge finish required, different thread types may be chosen: a spun polyester thread may be suggested for serging a mediumweight cotton fabric, but another choice may be to use a metallic yarn on the upper looper for a decorative effect. Refer to the sections on threads and decorative stitches for in-depth information on options available for tension setting and stitching methods.

Every serger comes with a manual that will suggest a needle system. For the best results, it is sensible to use the suggested needles and choose the thickness or size of needle to suit the weight of your fabric. This guide gives suggestions for needle size, but it should be used in conjunction with the information found in your machine's manual.

Not every machine will have settings to change differential feed and stitch length. Users of basic machines can use this fabric guide, but should ignore information for settings not available to them.

Lightweight fabrics

These may be sheer or opaque and vary in their pliability and softness. Some lightweight fabrics will fray more than others, which may affect the choice of seam or hem finish. Use a finer needle and shorter stitch length with these fabrics.

SEAMS
With sheer fabrics it is worth considering what the inside seam will look like, since this will most likely be visible from the outside of the garment. Delicate,

finer threads are preferable for such fabrics. Use either a 2- or 3-thread narrow serging stitch to create a fine finish.

HEMS
Rolled hems, picot edging, and narrow hemming work really well on lightweight fabrics, and it is much easier to finish these fabrics with a serger than to hem them on a standard sewing machine.

Roll hemming works brilliantly on chiffon and georgette fabrics.

TYPE OF FABRIC	THREAD TYPE	NEEDLE	STITCH LENGTH	DIFFERENTIAL FEED DIAL
Voile, georgette, crepe de chine, chiffon, cotton lawn	Cotton, silk or synthetic 80–100	70–80 (10–12)	2–3	0.5–1

Serge fine fabrics with just 2 or 3 threads for a more delicate finish.

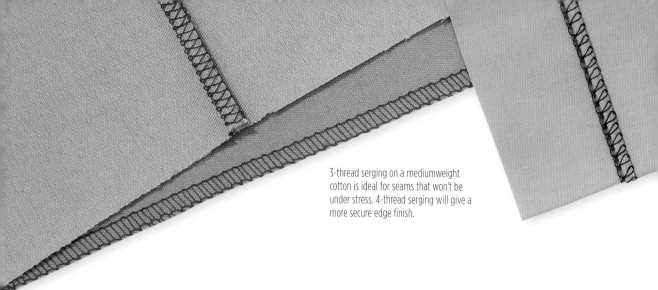

3-thread serging on a mediumweight cotton is ideal for seams that won't be under stress. 4-thread serging will give a more secure edge finish.

Mediumweight fabrics

Most easy-to-sew garment fabrics will come under this category. The techniques used for these fabrics depend on the purpose of the item being made.

SEAMS
A 3-thread serging stitch will be suitable for most mediumweight fabrics, but a 4-thread stitch can be used for added strength, depending on the purpose of the garment or item being made. Loosely woven fabrics will

benefit from being stitched on a sewing machine before serging to give extra strength and to avoid the serged edge being pulled off or raveling, creating holes in the seam. An alternative to this would be using a 4- or 5-thread safety stitch, which will have a similar appearance but be stronger.

HEMS
Narrow hemming can work well on some mediumweight fabrics,

depending on how much they fray. A 3-thread narrow hem or 3-thread serging stitch can be used here to good effect. Cover stitch can also be used if available on your serger, or simply serge first, turn under, press, and then stitch in place with your sewing machine. Try out samples using fabric scraps before committing to one technique.

TYPE OF FABRIC	THREAD TYPE	NEEDLE	STITCH LENGTH	DIFFERENTIAL FEED DIAL
Cotton, linen, satin, cotton blends, silk	Cotton or synthetic 60–100, silk 50-100	80–90 (12–14)	2.5–3.5	1

Heavyweight fabrics

A serger can add extra strength and durability to the seams and hems of heavyweight fabrics. Serging on the inside of pillows and other upholstery will ensure that these household items launder well without fraying in the wash. Make sure you use strong threads and thicker needles, otherwise some fabrics will not sew properly.

You may find that the serging pulls away from some tweeds and other woven fabrics every time you sew. Using a stabilizer or cotton stay tape may rectify this. If neither of these methods work, consider binding the seam allowances instead.

SEAMS

For heavy fabrics, first use the sewing machine and then serge with the maximum number of threads available on your serger model. Alternatively, for added strength, use a 4- or 5-thread safety stitch (if this is available on your machine). Heavyweight fabrics are usually bulky in the seams and so, depending on the purpose of your project, you may wish to sew first on a sewing machine and then serge each seam allowance separately. Test this out before trying it. For very bulky fabrics it may be easier to serge the edges first and then sew the seam on the sewing machine if the thickness

of the fabric and seams cannot be accommodated under the serger foot. An alternative to reducing bulkiness at seams is flatlocking, which can also be used as a decorative finish. Heavier fabrics may need a looser needle tension setting, too, so always test out your stitch on scrap fabrics first.

HEMS

Consider the thickness of the hem when choosing a finishing technique. Some thicker fabrics may look great with a 3- or 4-thread serged edge and others would look better serged, turned under, and stitched again, creating a cover stitch finish.

TYPE OF FABRIC	THREAD TYPE	NEEDLE	STITCH LENGTH	DIFFERENTIAL FEED DIAL
Denim, tweed, canvas, upholstery fabrics	Cotton, silk or synthetic 50–60	90–100 (14–16)	3–4	1

Serge heavy fabrics with 4 or 5 threads to ensure a secure finish. Use decorative threads to hem the edges of fabrics for simple tablecloths or throws.

Glossary

Balanced stitch
A stitch where the needle threads sit correctly on the top and underside of the fabric and the looper threads meet only at the very edge of the fabric.

Basting
Temporary stitching by hand or machine, using long stitches.

Bias
The diagonal across the fabric. True bias is at a 45° angle to any straight edge when the grains are perpendicular.

Bias binding
A strip of fabric cut on the bias. It can be wrapped over the edge of fabric to add a decorative trim to seams and hems.

Blind hem
An invisible or almost invisible hemming finish, where edges are finished and hemmed in one step. This technique works best on heavier fabrics such as upholstery fabrics, fleece, and wool.

Bodkin
A needle with a large eye that is sometimes sold as an embroidery needle for children. It may be plastic or metal with a blunt tip. Bodkins are great for finishing off the ends of serging.

Chain off
Stitching on the serger without fabric to create a chained end that can be cut using the thread cutter on the machine or scissors.

Chain stitch
A stitch formed with one looper and one needle. On the right side, the stitch looks like a straight stitch; on the reverse of the fabric, a chain is formed.

Chiffon
A sheer lightweight fabric.

Converter
Used for 2-thread serging stitches, this may be a separate item or attached to the upper looper of the machine. It blocks the eye of the upper looper, allowing the machine to work with just the lower looper and one needle.

Cover stitch
A double or triple row of parallel straight stitching on the top side of the fabric, with a serged finish on the underside. It is most commonly used to hem knitted fabrics, where it adds topstitching while at the same time finishing the raw edge on a hem.

Differential feed
This works in conjunction with the feed dog teeth and can be used to eliminate unwanted gathering, stretching, or puckering on seams and hems. It can also be used to create gathers and stretch where required. The differential feed controls the speed at which the feed dog teeth move.

Edge finishing
The raw edge of the fabric can be finished with pinking shears, zigzag stitch on a conventional sewing machine, or by serging the edge of the fabric.

Facing
A piece of fabric used to finish the unhemmed or unfinished edges of a garment. Facings are usually found on necklines, waistlines, and hems.

Fagoting
Where two pieces of fabric are joined together, leaving a gap in between. The gap can be filled with cover stitch or flatlocking.

Feed dog teeth
These teeth can be found below the presser foot. On a serger there are two sets of teeth that work with the differential feed. The teeth work independently of each other, one at the front guiding the fabric under the foot toward the needle and one at the rear of the machine taking the fabric from behind the needle.

Fell seam
Created by stitching on the sewing machine with wrong sides of the fabric together. One seam allowance is trimmed and the other folded over to enclose the trimmed seam allowance. This can then be finished by stitching again on the sewing machine or by using the cover stitch or chain stitch on the serger. Fell seams are great for adding additional strength to a garment or bag.

Flatlocking
Where two edges or a fold of fabric are serged and then pulled open so that the stitches lie flat. Flatlocking can be substituted for a regular serged seam to add detail to seam lines on the right side of a garment or bag. It works best on heavy or bulky fabrics that don't fray easily. The flatlock stitch is reversible and can be used on the right or wrong side of a project to show either loops or ladders.

Foot pedal
The pedal used to control the speed of the machine. The harder you press, the faster the machine goes. On some foot pedals you can change the speed setting to high or low, allowing you to work more slowly or more quickly, depending on your preference.

French seam
A type of self-enclosed seam where the seam allowances are all enclosed within the stitching. Because the seam is sewn twice it gives added strength to the stitching, making it more hardwearing. Stitch first with wrong sides together, press the seam to one side, and then fold right sides together and stitch again, enclosing the seam allowances or original serged seam.

Handwheel
Sometimes referred to as the flywheel. It can be turned by hand to move the position of the needles and loopers when changing the needle, threading the machine, or while stitching to ensure greater accuracy in where the stitches pierce the fabric. As a general rule, always turn the handwheel toward you.

Interfacing
A layer of fabric that supports, shapes, and stabilizes many areas of the garment. It is usually found in collars, cuffs, plackets, waistbands, facings, and around buttonholes. It may be fusible (iron-on) or non-fusible (sew-in) and comes in different weights in either black or white.

Jersey
Knitted stretch fabric made from a range of fibers.

Lettuce-leaf edge
A decorative frilled edge made by increasing the differential feed dial and using a short stitch length or satin stitch.

Lint
Fluff from fabrics and threads that builds up inside the machine.

Loop turner
A tool used for turning through stitching and seams to the right side, e.g., when creating rouleau loops or skinny straps for clothing, bags, or other household items.

Looper
The serger generally has two loopers, an upper and a lower one, which work together to carry threads from side to side to wrap the edge of the fabric.

Looper cover
A cover on the machine to encase the loopers. On some machines there are two and on others just one. Some machines have a safety device that stops the machine from stitching if the looper covers are open.

Mock band hem
A hem that resembles a band stitched to the edge of the fabric.

Needle plate
Found under the presser foot, this provides a smooth surface that passes the fabric under the foot of the machine. It has a hole for the needle and the feed dog teeth.

Picot edge
A decorative edging formed on the serger by combining roll hemming and a long stitch length. The hem resembles a scalloped edge and works best on medium- or lightweight fabrics.

Pin tucks
Narrow rows of tucks formed by using rolled hem, cover stitch, or chain stitch settings.

Piping
Cord wrapped with bias binding used to form decorative seams.

Pivot
A term used to describe turning the fabric while the needle is holding it in position at the machine.

Press
When you stitch a seam, you must press it to set or embed the stitches and then press the seam allowance either open or to one side to make the seam lie flat. Pressing is very different to ironing: when you iron clothes, you move the iron backward and forward; when you press a seam, you lower the iron onto the fabric and then lift it up again—this avoids distorting the threads and pulling the piece out of shape.

Presser foot
This holds the fabric flat as it is fed through the machine. A basic serger foot is provided with the machine and will do most types of serging.

Roll hemming
A very narrow stitch that rolls the fabric to the underside as it is sewn. It is used to create a hem or add detail to a garment. This type of stitch works best on light- to mediumweight fabrics to create a delicate yet strong edge finish. The stitch is formed from the right needle and one or two loopers. Set the right needle slightly tighter than normal and tighten the lower looper thread. The lower looper thread will pull the upper looper thread to the back of the fabric, rolling the fabric edge at the same time.

Rouleau loop
Generally narrow cordlike strips of fabric that can be used as straps, button loops, ties, and other decoration. Formed by cutting and stitching bias strips with right sides together and then turning through to the right side.

Satin stitch
Close stitching formed using a really short stitch length. This gives better coverage when creating narrow or roll hemming or when covering cord.

Sealant
This stops seams from fraying or serge chains from raveling. Use sparingly and always test a section first.

Seam allowance
The amount of fabric between the stitching or seam line and the edge of fabric—usually ⅝in (1.5cm).

Seams
A stitched line joining two pieces of fabric.

Sheer
Transparent or see-through.

Shirring
A way of gathering fabric using thin cord elastic stitched in rows.

Slipstitch
A hand-sewing stitch used to close a seam or stitch a hem where the stitching is invisible from the right side.

Spool
A cylinder onto which thread is wound.

Stabilizer
Backing fabric used to add strength to a seam or fabric edge. The stabilizer may be ironed in place before a seam is sewn or may be dissolvable so that it can be removed once stitching is complete.

Stitch finger
Also called a stitch former, a small piece of metal around which the stitch is formed. Usually found on the needle plate. To enable narrower stitching or roll hemming, it can usually be disengaged and moved out of the way.

Tension
How tightly or loosely the thread is held and pulled through the machine.

Thread guide bar
This keeps the threads untangled as they travel from the spool to the machine. The bar can be extended and should be raised up to its highest position to allow the threads to travel smoothly.

Thread guides
These hold the thread in place as it goes from the spool to its location on the machine, either to a needle or to a looper.

Topstitching
Machine stitching sewn from the right side of the fabric for decoration or strength. This may be done on the serger using the chain stitch or cover stitch settings.

Twill tape
Used to strengthen a seam and prevent it from stretching. Often used at a waistline and made of non-stretch fabric.

Welt seam
Created by stitching on the sewing machine with right sides of the fabric together. One seam allowance is trimmed and the other folded over, covering the trimmed seam allowance. This can then be finished by serging the untrimmed seam allowance and stitching again on the sewing machine, or using the cover stitch or chain stitch on the serger. Welt seams are great for adding additional strength to a garment or bag.

Index

Credits

Quarto would like to thank and acknowledge the following for supplying images for inclusion in this book:

Feng Yu, Shutterstock, p.16tl (1)
Stephen Rees, Shutterstock, p.16tl (2)
Urfin, Shutterstock, p.120l

All other photographs and illustrations are the copyright of Quarto Publishing plc. While every effort has been made to credit contributors, Quarto would like to apologize should there have been any omissions or errors—and would be pleased to make the appropriate correction for future editions of the book.

Quarto are grateful to Janome who kindly supplied the sergers used in this book. www.janome.com.

Author's acknowledgements
A huge thanks to Margaret Hincks, my mom, for all the help with creating samples, finding fabrics, talking through ideas, and for passing on your sewing skills. I couldn't have done this without you.

Thanks also to Elizabeth Betts at Quilty Pleasures for your help with choosing fabrics and batting for the quilt project, and for opening up just for me on your day off. www.quilty-pleasures.co.uk.